GOD, SEX and KABBALAH
RABBI ALLEN S. MALLER

Y0-BBW-720

GOD, SEX
AND
KABBALAH

(MESSIANIC SPECULATIONS)

by

RABBI ALLEN S. MALLER

The author gratefully acknowledges and Thanks *Rabbi Zalman Schechter* for permission to use his "The First Step"

For additional copies of his book, write to:
Rabbi/Akiba, 5249 S. Sepulveda Blvd., Culver City, CA 90230

Library of Congress Catalog Card Number: 82-12318

ISBN—0-86628-019-7

Copyright © 1983
Rabbi Allen S. Maller
Los Angeles, California

All rights reserved. No part of this publication may be reproduced, stored in a retrieval system or transmitted in any form by any means, electronic, mechanical, photocopying, recording or otherwise, without the prior permission in writing from the publisher.

This book is dedicated to **Ann Lowenkoph** for helping me to write, and my wife, **Judith,** for helping me to feel, and to the members of **Temple Akiba** for making me proud to be a Rabbi.

CONTENTS

FOREWARNING

Books usually begin with a foreword to lure the readers. This book begins with a forewarning: proceed with caution. Unless the need to realize the meaning of life nags at you, don't proceed at all. The subject matter of this book may not be comfortable. It may seethe within and change your life.

This is the Kabbalah, the Jewish mystical tradition that deals with the spiritual forces that are within and yet beyond our five senses. Originally, thousands of years ago, it was forbidden to write down the words of the Kabbalah. The masters of the Kabbalah kept their powers and their knowledge hidden from the community, lest the unready be tempted to reach out and harm themselves. Kabbalistic knowledge was passed down from each mystic, to one or two carefully selected disciples. In this way each teacher personally knew his students and could judge what was appropriate for them to learn, what they could understand, and how fast they should advance in their studies.

Between the twelfth and seventeenth centuries, opposition to writing down the Kabbalah weakened and dozens of Kabbalistic books appeared. Still, students were prohibited from studying these texts until they had been thoroughly grounded in the Bible, with its commentaries and interpretations, as well as the Talmuds' 63 volumes of Jewish law and lore, and before their personal lives had matured sufficiently to sustain them through the stress of their studies.

The student of the Kabbalah faces the hidden knowledge of God's creation and the nature of the Deity. This knowledge can unleash powerful forces that may be used or misused depending upon the character, moral strength, and maturity of the individual. Traditional evidence points out that masters of certain aspects of the Kabbalah can transcend the usual laws of nature. Even students who reject the temptation to use Kabbalistic knowledge as a source of power, may face emotional explosions from within, or without, that become progressively overwhelming as one approaches Deity.

When people who are not firmly rooted in the scientific, rational, and traditional disciplines of the Jewish community study the Kabbalah, there is the danger that what they absorb may corrupt them, and expose them to experiences beyond their ability to withstand or control. Even the great Kabbalist, Rabbi Judah Loew, of Prague, was almost overcome by this danger when a creation of his threatened to destroy an entire city (see "The Golem of Rabbi Loew"). If a mature, deeply rooted mind like his, faced such a problem, how much the more so would it be true of the thousands of young people today, who drift from place to place, seeking and searching. We who live in the last half of the twentieth century, in the shadow of the atomic bomb, and the likelihood that our own wastes are poisoning the world, have learned that terrible dangers are inherent in the use of power, even when it is intended for good.

Why then this book about Kabbalah for the general public? Different times create different necessities. Today, there is an awakening among young people to the spiritual realities inside and beyond them. There is a great deal of interest in extrasensory perception, the control of brain waves, yoga, meditation, and mystical experiences and exercises of all types. However, those who are adept in the mysteries of the Kabbalah still do not teach them openly. And those who openly attempt to teach the Kabbalah rarely know much about their subject. Frequently they are not even Jewish. Usually they are not able to read the Aramaic and Hebrew languages in which the texts of the Kabbalah were originally written. There are more than 12,000 written works on Kabbalah. Three quarters of these exist only as handwritten, unpublished manuscripts. Of the more than 3,000 printed texts, only one or two dozen have ever been translated into English. Thus for people who do not read and understand rabbinic Hebrew as well as Aramaic, 99.8% of the Kabbalistic literature will forever remain closed and hidden.

This is as it should be. Those who are not grounded in the Talmud, the centuries of Biblical interpretation of the Torah, and the Prophets, cannot possibly teach Kabbalah correctly. Yet many teachers and pseudo-teachers, holy men from other faiths, and businessmen in saffron robes, are responding to the interest in spirituality with the devices of mass media. Quicky religious transplants are being attempted for innocent young people, without consideration of the danger of imposing one person's religion from a foreign culture, on another person's being. These people promise that with this mantra, or that chant, their followers can find truth, ultimate reality, their real selves, or the highest illumination. Too often, after a period of euphoria, the result is spiritual chaos, emotional disorientation, and further alienation from family and community.

In the medieval Jewish community, students had to abide by the decision of the community regarding the limitations on their studying the Kabbalah because there were no other mystical sources available to them, and because the pressure of the community was very strong. Today, with a world of places and persons beckoning, enthusiasm and impatience can draw sincere students onto barren or dangerous paths. Therefore, it seems necessary to offer an explanation of some aspects of the Jewish mystical experience in the past, and in the present, so that individuals will have the opportunity to learn enough about the authentic Kabbalah to dismiss false teaching and misinterpretations, and to judge whether they wish to undergo the discipline of further study.

Finally, in the next few decades, our growing scientific sophistication will enable us to communicate with intelligent beings in other solar systems. This represents a further development of the Messianic Age which we have already entered. Before we can communicate with intelligent beings on other worlds, we need to improve our communication with the intelligent beings in our own world. An increase in human spirituality and an exploration of inner space is necessary to prepare us for the developments of the twenty-first century. The Kabbalistic concepts of Tsimtsum and Tikun will enable us to understand the true meaning of contact with extraterrestial life (see "Intelligent Life in Outer Space").

This book is designed to reflect the character and personality of the various elements in the Kabbalah. It contains stories, interpretations of Bible and Jewish history, prophecies of future developments, translations of famous Kabbalistic texts, meditation exercises; and an advocacy of performing the mitzvot, without which no book of Kabbalah can be considered authentic. The purpose of this book is to be a beginning: to provide the reader with an introduction to the various aspects of Kabbalah in order that the reader may determine which path to pursue in raising his or her spiritual consciousness.

The chapters do not have to be read in strict order. You may use your own intuition to select which chapters to read first and which to read later. I have organized the chapters as follows: chapter I recounts the events and issues surrounding the creation of a Golem by Rabbi Judah Loew. Chapter II presents the background of the two most important texts in Kabbalistic literature, the Zohar and the Sefer Yetzirah. The next chapter deals with a particular type of Kabbalistic code called Gematria. Chapters IV-VII deal with the role of the female in Jewish mystical thought. The holy significance of sexual intercourse, the role of woman in man's ascent from the Garden of Eden, the image of the female as God, and as demon, are all dealt with.

Chapters VIII and IX present views of what happens after death. For most readers, especially for those who think they already know what Judaism teaches about this, these chapters will be shocking, and I hope enlightening. Chapters X and XI present various insights about the meaning of Jewish history, the purpose of Jewish survival, and the destiny of the Jewish people. Although these themes are important ones in Kabbalah, they are rarely, if ever, treated in books written for the general public. The chapter on the coming of the Messianic Age naturally leads to Chapter XII which discusses the period after the Messianic Age, which I believe will see us come into contact with intelligent life in outer space. Chapters XIII and XIV show you how to begin your own practice of meditation and spiritual exercise.

Finally Chapter XV ends in the same way as this book begins; with a warning to those who seek mystical experience; not all Books on Kabbalah are Kosher. Those I recommend and those I do not recommend are listed.

Amulet for childbirth: The two triangles are interlaced to form a hexagram within a circle.

Circumference: Adam and Eve, Hutz, Lilith, the First Eve. Shamriel, Hasdiel, Sinvai and Sansanvai and Semanglof. Fourteen-letter Name. Ps. 91:11. Amen, Selah.

Around hexagram: The 42-letter Name.

In hexagon: Exodus 11:8.

In the name of Kuph—(six anagrammatic forms).

Outside the circle: The four Rivers of Paradise. (From *Sefer Raziel* Ed. 1701, p. 43a).

THE GOLEM OF RABBI LOEW

During the sixteenth century, Rabbi Judah Loew was inspired by the Lord to be an agent of deliverance for the Jewish people. By the very act of being born, he saved the Jewish community of his town from bloody destruction. It happened in this fashion:

It was the Eve of the Passover. The Loew family had invited their relatives and several friends to join them at the Seder table. The service had no sooner begun than the mother, in her ninth month with child, went into deep labor pains. Her husband jumped up and ran out into the night to find a doctor. And, quickly, the other men at the table joined him, each going in a different direction. In those days hospitals were rare even in large cities, and doctors were few and often could be located only by searching house to house following the trail of the sick and injured they had treated.

In the ghetto, the streets were empty and deserted. Everyone was indoors for the Seder as they always are in every Jewish community on the Eve of the Passover. For this reason, one of the guests was surprised to come upon a stranger scurrying down a street, keeping to the shadows. Visibly startled by the sound of footsteps, the stranger ducked into an alley, quickening his pace. His burst of speed and furtive behavior made the guest suspicious. On impulse, he changed direction hastening to catch up to the stranger who, upon looking over his shoulder, realized he was being followed. Sweating and wheezing for breath, the stranger pulled something from under his jacket and threw it down, continuing to flee as fast as he could.

The guest, thinking the stranger was a thief, pounced on the object. It was wrapped in a tallit — a prayer shawl. He unrolled the tallit and found the dead body of a tiny baby. Horrified, the guest stared numbly down at the dead baby for a few minutes, before the significance of the small body struck him. During this period the Jews often were accused by their enemies of killing Christian babies to drain their blood for the baking of Matzah, or the making of wine for the Seder meal. Ironically, this was similar to the charge the Romans made against the Christians when

Christian-baiting was a prime diversion of the Roman Empire. Now, in their turn, Christian anti-Semites used the lie to incite ignorant peasants to attack the Jewish community.

This charge against the Jews had been denounced by the Pope himself, who declared the Jewish people innocent of such atrocities. But blatant lies always have been a tool used by wicked men. Then, as now, fanatics and haters were looking for an excuse, any excuse, to vomit out the poisonous emotions festering within them.

This anti-Semitic plot was surprisingly simple to effect. It was a time when babies, Christian and Jewish, died more often than they lived. Their corpses were easy to find. The same script had been acted out many times before and usually with success. Agents of a conspiracy against the Jews, entered a ghetto and placed a corpse of a Christian baby in the cellar of a prominent Jew, or in the basement of a Synagogue. Then the conspirators arranged for a search and discovery, spreading the news of the event, and inflaming the resulting terror and rage among the Christians to incite a pogrom — a massacre of Jewish people which swept through the countries of Europe in periodic surges like a plague.

The guest covered the body gently with the tallit, and ran back to the Loew house where a doctor was already at the mother's side, helping with the birth of the baby destined to be Rabbi Loew. After a hurried conference, the men took the corpse to the local authorities and described how they had found it. The identity of the agent who had sneaked into their community was never discovered, but the plot itself was aborted, and the conspirators were forced, at least for a time, to leave the Jewish community in peace.

So little Judah had already earned the gratitude of his community for saving them from a pogrom before he had first been placed in his mother's arms, and he was marked as one chosen to be a defender of the Jewish people.

He grew up demonstrating unusual brilliance in the study of the Talmud, the Torah, and the Kabbalah. As a young man he was ordained a rabbi and served the community at Nicholsberg for twenty years. He married late, at thirty-two, but in time to have seven children, six daughters and one son. It is said that the study of the Kabbalah can either shorten one's life or lengthen it: Rabbi Judah Loew lived to the age of ninety-seven, dying in 1609.

While he was still a relatively young man, during his twentieth year at Nicholsberg, Rabbi Judah had been invited to assume the important position of head of the Jewish community in Prague in what is now

Czechoslovakia and was then Bohemia, and he and his family moved there in 1574. It was while he was in Prague that the events of this story took place.

It happened that at that time a priest by the name of Thaddeus lived in the city of Prague. Jewish customs were strange to him and anything strange made him uneasy. Further, the Jews did not contribute work or wealth to his church, and this aroused his anger. Anger slowly had soured into hatred, because whenever he tried to persuade the Jews to accept Christ as their Messiah, for every argument he made, they always had an answer. And of all the Jews, the fury of Thaddeus the priest centered on Rabbi Judah Loew for reasons that you are about to hear.

In those days there lived in Prague Michael Berger, a wine dealer, whose only child, Rachael, had just reached the age of seventeen years. The wine dealer had a reputation for courtesy and honesty which had brought him a large clientele and a comfortable livelihood. Among his customers was Thaddeus, the priest. During the year that Rachael had changed from a child to a lovely young woman, Thaddeus had become obsessed with the desire to convert her to Christianity. He told himself that he wanted to save her soul, but he could not keep his eyes off Rachael as she waited on her father's customers. If only he could pluck this young beauty from the faith of her fathers, he felt it would make up for all the arguments he had lost. And the thought of teaching Rachael the catechism sent a warm wave of pleasure through his body.

After many months of scheming, Thaddeus decided on a plan of action. One day when he knew Michael Berger would be absent, Thaddeus stormed into the wine shop with a show of angry complaint about the quality of the last shipment of wine he had received. As he expected, Rachael defended her father and the quality of his wine.

"Come to my house", the priest challenged. "Taste the wine for yourself and I will leave it to your judgment".

Rachael, who saw the world through the goodness she knew at home, agreed. At his house, Thaddeus opened a bottle of wine and gave her a glass. She drank it and said there was nothing wrong with it. Thaddeus sipped from the little he had poured himself and reluctantly agreed, exclaiming that it must have been one of the other bottles that was bad. He repeated his performance with a second bottle; and a third. One by one, pretending to be looking angrily for the offending wine, Thaddeus handed Rachael glasses full of wine from different bottles until the entire ten bottles of his shipment stood on the table, all of them sampled.

By then Thaddeus could see from the pink flush on Rachael's cheeks that the wine had begun to warm her body and muddle her mind. He started to talk softly of other things than wine. He described the life at the Polish court, making it sound exciting and gay. He told her of the day he had been presented to the King of Bohemia. He discussed with easy familiarity the nobles of his parish and their castles, the cathedrals of Prague, their works of art and angelic choirs, the colorful costumes of the prelates of the Church and the rich lives they led. When Rachael finally left for home, her head was buzzing with the priest's tales. On her return to her father's shop, for the first time it seemed small and drab.

Again and again, Thaddeus arranged to catch Rachael alone in the shop and linger after his purchases, talking of palace balls and church pageants. banquets, morality plays, and Christian art. Rachael listened, her eyes wide and shining with excitement. But when her father returned and asked her. as he always did, what had happened in his absence, she never mentioned the priest's words, not connecting them with her growing sense of dissatisfaction. Within her heart she knew her father would not want her to talk at length to the priest. Obscurely she felt guilty about both the conversations and her failure to mention them to her father, although she told herself angrily that she was old enough now to know how to talk to customers, and not have to report every little exchange to her parents.

As the weeks went by, Rachael became short-tempered. Her parent's life seemed degrading and monotonous compared to the world of the Christians as romanticized by Thaddeus. His hints that she could slip into that world by becoming a Christian added guilt and anger to her dissatisfaction, because increasingly they tempted her.

One day after a particularly long and dazzling conversation, Rachael burst out crying. Thaddeus murmured that a drive in the fresh air would cheer her up. He coaxed her into his elegant carriage, telling his coachman on the sly to drive them to a certain monastery. As the horses slowly clomped down the cobbled streets, Thaddeus used his experience with young people to build up resentment in Rachael against her family. convincing her that the emotional turmoil she was feeling was fatigue brought on by overwork in her father's shop and too little recreation. He argued persuasively that her confusion was the first pullings of desire to put her faith in Christ. When, at last, the carriage stopped in front of the monastery, Thaddeus urged the now nearly hysterical young woman to stay there a few days so she could rest and be alone to pray and think.

Repressing a sinking feeling that she was doing the worst thing she had ever done in her life, Rachael gave herself over to weeping and allowed the priest to lead her into the monastery. Gleefully, Thaddeus returned to the shop and told Michael Berger his daughter would not return home that night and why, gloating over the pain and fear in the wine merchant's eyes.

Michael Berger begged the priest to be allowed to enter the monstery and talk with his daughter if only for a few moments. Of course, knowing how frail his hold over Rachael was, the priest refused. At length, the frantic father went to the civil authorities with the story, pleading with them to restore his daughter, or at least to force Thaddeus to grant him permission to visit her. However, the civil authorities claimed that they could not interfere with church affairs.

In order to make his own position stronger, Thaddeus went to one of his parishioners, a count, suggesting the possibility of a marriage between Rachael and the count's handsome younger son. Thaddeus pointed out that the Church would find ways to reward the man responsible for the conversion of a Jew. He hinted that Rachael's father had more wealth than one might think from his simple way of life. And, he promised, Rachael would grace the count's family as she was both beautiful and modest.

After seeing the girl for himself, the count agreed that the two young people should meet. At their first meeting, the count's son, Ladislaus, fell under the spell of Rachael's beauty and charm. She, too, was overwhelmed, by the glamour of this blond noble whose carefree air was so different from the men of the ghetto. Before the day was over, the count and Thaddeus were certain that the young couple would agree to their plans.

The two men decided on a wedding date two months from that day. But the wedding was to be preceded by Rachael's conversion, which would take place in the great cathedral of Prague. Perhaps, Thaddeus told Rachael, who was looking increasingly uneasy as the talk centered around her conversion, the king might agree to be her godfather. And to distract her further, he promised that the sweethearts could meet every day until the marriage, provided that they were properly chaperoned.

When Rachael's parents learned that their only child was engaged to marry a non-Jew, they were distraught. The chain of generations would be broken. Their ancestors had stood at Mount Sinai when the Covenant was forged between God and the Jewish people. That Covenant was not just for those standing there so long ago; it was for the generations to come. Ninety five generations of Jews had carried on the ways of their people, including the honoring of that Covenant, down to their time. And, it seemed, that their daugther was going to break the link. Their grandchildren would be raised as Christians and would not know the Jewish way or the Covenant of the Jewish people. Who knows? They thought, their own grandchildren might someday be among the anti-

Semites. It had happened before in cases like this. What could they do? How could they reach out to Rachael and bring her to realize the terrible thing she was doing?

They felt helpless to avert the tragedy. The count was too powerful a figure to oppose. And, they discovered, it was equally impossible to reason with him. In desperation they turned to Rabbi Loew, praying that somehow he might be able to help. After several minutes of silent consideration, Rabbi Loew asked them, "If Rachael were released from the monastery, do you have a distant relative with whom she would be safe?"

"Oh yes," Michael Berger assured him. "I have a brother in Amsterdam. He would welcome Rachael into his household."

Smiling to himself, Rabbi Loew cautioned the parents to say nothing to anyone about coming to him for help. Two weeks later, Ladislaus the count's son, received news from the monastery of the sudden death of his fiancee. Grief struck deep at his heart. He shut himself up in his room, refusing to eat or even to take a sip of wine. His father brought one after another of the daughters of noble families to visit Ladislaus, hoping to find one who could make him stop grieving for Rachael.

But day by day, Ladislaus grew more silent and withdrawn. His courtship of Rachael, brief as it had been, had changed him. He had learned that a relationship between a man and a woman could mean more than the quick rush of blood of a flirtation and the prestige of wearing a lovely woman on his arm. He could not shake Rachael from his memory. As the weeks and months went by, he realized that those aspects of Rachael which he loved most stemmed from her Jewish heritage. Her liveliness, the emotional intensity and vivacity with which she met life, her concern with social justice, and her interest in ideas. Unlike the women he had met at court, Rachael was not trained to be meek, calculating, or coldly formal and dull. She was warm, spontaneous, verbal, and honest. He decided if ever he were to marry, it could only be with another Jewish girl.

Lladislaus thought of the possibility of Thaddeus once more succeeding to convert a Jewish girl and recoiled, remembering the times Rachael had sobbed against his shoulder at the prospect of her forthcoming conversion. He remembered, too, Rachael's stories of the cooperation and closeness and warmth among the Jews of the ghetto. He did not want to wrench someone he loved away from the wonderful life Rachael had described. Suddenly Ladislaus realized. . . he wanted to become a Jew.

The realization brought him a jolt of fear. Becoming a Jew was against the law. Even more dangerous were the ways that the Church would retaliate. Men had been tortured and burned at the stake for less. He would endanger the lives of both his family and the Jewish community he wished to join by going to one of rabbis of Prague for religious instruction. But Ladislaus was a stubborn young man. He decided if he were too well known to join the Jewish community at home, he would try elsewhere. Keeping his resolve secret, he arranged to tour the European countries, a practice fashionable then as now. He travelled from town to town, in one country after another, seeking a rabbi to teach him how to join the Jewish people. Again and again he was turned away by rabbis who either were afraid to risk what little security their communities knew, or who looked into the young man's heart and decided his resolve to become a Jew had not fully ripened yet.

Finally, Ladislaus met a rabbi who consented to begin his religious instruction. He studied hard and prayed intently. Finally after several months, his teacher told him the time had come when he could be accepted into a Jewish community, but it was too dangerous to do so formally in his town. The Rabbi handed Ladislaus a letter of introduction, telling him to go to Amsterdam, which enjoyed greater religious freedom than any other city in Europe. "There," the rabbi told Ladislaus, "you can continue your studies in the Torah. The rabbinical schools of Amsterdam are among the best in the world."

Ladislaus had been studyng for two years at the Yeshiva in Amsterdam when his master advised him to begin thinking about mariage, telling him it was not respectable for a man to be single after the age of thirty. Yeshurun—for that was the name given Ladislaus in his adopted faith—asked his master to help him meet a young woman he might marry, although in his heart he still did not feel ready to commit himself to a new relationship.

One day his master came to Yeshurun with the news that he had persuaded one of the men in their community, Hayim Berger, to allow a meeting between his niece and Yeshurun. As his master excitedly began to describe the niece, Yeshurun felt a stir of interest, and he agreed to a meeting.

When the two young people were brought face to face, they could not believe the testimony of their eyes. But it was true. The impossible had happened. The two lovers had found each other. In Yeshurun's arms, Rachael sobbed out her story. She had been held a virtual prisoner at the monastery, kept from any contact with her family. Nevertheless, as the date for her baptism grew nearer, she realized how vain and foolish she had been. She knew she could not live as a Christian even to be the wife of the man she had come to love. She did not know what to do.Guilt over the pain she was causing her parents made her ashamed to go home. She was afraid to run away. In those days, the person of a woman unprotected by her family and community was not safe on the streets, not even for a few days. Remorse, misery, and hopelessness kept her from realizing how simple it would be, really, to return home and tell her parents she was sorry. Increasingly depressed, agitated, unable to sleep, one seemingly endless night she made an attempt on her life.

The monks discovered her in time. Hurriedly they sent out for their doctor, but, as fate would have it, he had been taken from home by another emergency. Fearing for Rachael's life, the brother brought back another doctor, a Jew. This man not only knew Rachael, he loved her as his own. He had delivered her himself and watched her grow from a red, wrinkled baby into a lovely young woman. He was horrified at Rachael's emotional state, which was far more serious than her physical condition. As soon as he left the monastery, he hurried to Rabbi Loew for advice. Together, the two men worked out a plan to rescue the girl.

Under the pretext of treating Rachael, the doctor gave her a drug that slowed her bodily responses to a point resembling death. Then, after telling the monks his patient had died, the doctor removed the "corpse" from the monastery and bribed a gravedigger to act out a burial. As soon as Rachael revived from the drug, Rabbi Loew smuggled her out of the country, sending her to her uncle, Michael Berger's brother, in Amsterdam.

So, after an ordeal that lasted almost three years, to the joy of her parents and Yeshurun's teachers, Rachael and Yeshurun were married under the hupa—the ceremonial canopy covering a bride and groom during a Jewish wedding. Despite the need for secrecy, the reunion of the count's son and the wine merchant's daughter, was too good a story to be kept quiet. It spread from one family to the next, finally reaching Prague, where inevitably, it came to the ears of Thaddeus.

The priest realized that not only had he failed in his ambition to convert Rachael, but, through his scheming, he had lost one of his own parishioners to Judaism. The king and his bishop would be furious with him and he would be exposed to the ridicule of his enemies. Hatred of the Jews and of Rabbi Judah Loew raged within him. His fulminations from the pulpit against the Jews became increasingly hysterical. The whispers and sly smiles which seemed to surround him continually fanned the flames of his fury. Finally when Easter and the Passover approached, Thaddeus remembered the blood libel against the Jews and saw a way to have his revenge. He began a whisper campaign that the Jews were planning to kidnap Christian babies to slaughter them for the Seder meal.

There were two factions among the Christians who eagerly seized upon the story to use against each other. The struggle between the Reformation and the Counter—Reformation in Bohemia had reached a furious peak during this period. Catholics and Protestants continually broke the peace with internecine skirmishes, each accusing the other of all manner of charges, including hidden Jewish leanings. Not caring if innocents were hurt in the process, both sides spread the story to bolster the onslaughts of their own propaganda. At the same time, nobles and businessmen in debt to Jewish money-lenders backed the story, hoping for a bloodbath against the Jews that would wash away their debts.

As Passover neared, tension and hostility mounted. A pogrom seemed inevitable. The least incident would start the bloodshed. Rabbi Judah Loew was in an agony of fear for his people's safety. He spent a long cold night praying and when morning came, bleak and grey, he finally decided to use his powers to make a Golem.

Now the mysteries of Practical Kabbalah were an open book to Rabbi Loew. However, he was extremely reluctant to apply his knowledge. Only for such an emergency as this would he take his attention away from the greater wonder of God, to use the powers which often have harmed men's bodies and corrupted their character. Despite his misgivings, when evening came, he gathered his assistant and his son-in-law, Yitzchok, and hurriedly led them from the ghetto to the banks of the river. By one o'clock the next morning, they were on their knees on the riverbank forming the figure of a man from wet clay. They worked hastily, driven by fear that at any moment, they might hear the first shouts of the pogrom.

Of necessity, as they formed the figure of mud, they made him lying on his back. But without their realizing it, in that position, their perspective of him was distorted. They were almost done before Rabbi Loew began to suspect that he had sculpted the form too large. And, indeed, the figure was a giant's size, at least seven feet tall, and more than four hundred pounds in weight. Once the man was completely formed, Rabbi Loew wrote the name of God—Yhvh—on a piece of parchment and placed it into the ear of the clay figure. He then uttered, in perfect pronunciation and true accent, God's holy Name.

Thick clouds had blown over the moon while they had been at work. The night had grown black. It was difficult to see their man of clay clearly, but he lay as they had made him, unmoving. The three men stood silently. . . waiting. Time, too, seemed to wait.

Overhead, a streak of lightning broke through the clouds, crashing down by the river not far from where they stood. The blinding flash was followed by a thunderous roar which caused the three men to fall to the ground. Even Rabbi Judah Loew was terrified at that moment, thinking perhaps he had gone too far; perhaps it was wrong to use his power to create marvels even to save his people. He knew of the warnings against using the Kabbalah for mundane affairs. He knew the danger of creation.

Limply, the three men remained on the ground where they had fallen in a state of shock. At last the lightning stopped, the storm loosed its rain, and the falling drops cleared their heads., As the rain poured down on them, the men scrambled to their feet, not noticing at first that there were four figures standing by the river. Rabbi Judah Loew turned and saw a giant figure moving toward him in the darknes. Barely able to breathe, he managed to gasp out the words, "Golem, stand still."

The figure stopped. The three men gathered around it wonderingly. In their excitement, they no longer noticed the rain pelting down on them, or the trickles of water that were starting to wash against their boots. They looked up at this massive creature towering above them. A creature they had made from clay. They looked and were filled with awe.

"Let us thank God," said Rabbi Judah Loew at last, and he began intoning the Blessing which is said on special occasions: Shehekiyanu.

The Blessing restored his composure. The rabbi faced the Golem and ordered him to follow after them. Then, Rabbi Loew turned, and with his assistants, retraced their way back to the ghetto. As they walked, Yitzchok, his son-in-law, asked him how he could be sure the Golem would continue to obey his commands and if the giant would be able to help them defeat their enemies.

The rabbi thought quietly for awhile and then answered, "The danger in creation is that the creation soon acquires a life of its own. That leads to a degree of independent action. It is clear that even God Himself had to give man independence in order for man to become man. Every day we see that when a child grows up, he slowly ceases to do everything his parents, who after all are his mortal creators, desire of him. Artists who create a work often report that their creations seem to acquire a kind of personality of their own, and seem to lead instead of being led. We shall have to be very, very careful if we are to maintain our control over this Golem.

"As for your second question, we can easily discover the answer to that."The rabbi pointed to a large branch on a nearby tree, saying commandingly, "Golem, break that off!"

The Golem misunderstood the rabbi's intention. He left the rabbi's side and began wrestling with the tree trunk. As he pushed and pulled at the huge trunk, the whole tree shook and Yitzchok began to laugh nervously.

Suddenly with a tremendous wrench of his powerful legs, the Golem freed the tree from the earth, lifting it high in the air, dirt from its roots showering down on the men below. Then the Golem brought the trunk of the tree over his knee. The trunk gave a loud cracking sound and splintered into two pieces. His mission accomplished, the Golem stood, one-half of the tree in either hand, waiting for further orders.

Yitzchok said in a hushed voice, "He's ten times stronger than the strongest man I've ever seen!" Nodding his head, his father-in-law repeated thoughtfully, "We must be very, very careful."

When the four returned to the ghetto, the rabbi led the Golem into the Synagogue's attic and ordered him to stay there. The next day he asked his wife to make some clothes for a newcomer to the ghetto, a giant of a man. His wife made a pair of pants, a shirt, and a jacket without question, although she wondered at the sizes her husband had described. After helping the Golem to dress himself, the rabbi led him down to the Synagogue and introduced him the community.

"This is Joseph," he said. "Joseph is a deaf-mute. He is a hard worker and will be happy to act as a water-carrier for us. If, at any time, there is a problem concerning Joseph the Golem, come to me. I know how to communicate with him through signs."

The people looked uneasily at this giant of a man, his complexion ruddy as the clay the potters dug up from the riverbank, his silent, passive face. If anyone but Rabbi Judah Loew had introduced him, they would have refused to accept him into their community. After a few days, however, their nervousness disappeared. They almost began to think of the Golem as one of themselves. Even the children stopped running away when he walked down the streets, carrying on his shoulders a water barrel for one of their homes.

There are many legends told of the Golem's deeds during this time, the feats of strength he performed, the missions he accomplished for Rabbi Loew. But I will speak only of the end of the Golem, for in its creation and in its destruction resides the insight into the power of the Kabbalah.

Well aware that Passover was almost upon him, Thaddeus continued to work feverishly. He had met privately with a number of the nobility who were badly in debt to Jewish bankers and moneylenders. Having laid the groundwork, he brought them together in a session filled with indirection and sanctimonious hypocrisy, and extracted from them a promise that the government would not interfere "if good Christian citizens attempt to drive this pernicious influence from our city."

Later he used this promise, coupled with his influence at court, to intimidate the Bishop, a kindly man, and, in fact, a personal friend of Rabbi Loew, but also a passive man, afraid to risk his own position in the Church by opposing a dangerous fanatic who had powerful friends.

Finally, by spreading around money belonging to the Church, Thaddeus had accumulated through his agents a small army of cutthroats, ruffians, drunks, and bullies who looked forward to the opportunity of looting and venting their frustrations on the persons of helpless women and children.

The people of Prague had not been told what would happen and when, but there was a smell of blood in the air. They kept their silence, some from cowardice and some smirking at the prospect of vicariously venting their hatred in violence. On Easter Sunday, which came before Passover that year, the pogrom began. Thaddeus ignited it in the morning, thundering from his pulpit, "The Christ-killers are living among us, rich and comfortable, flaunting their disbelief in our Lord. They endanger the Christian purity of our children, and their presence is an affront to the wounds of Christ, who died for our sins."

The congregation left his church muttering that the Jews should be driven from Prague. The men Thaddeus had hired mingled among them distributing liquor, urging secret action. As the people drank, their talk grew hot and more reckless. Soon they became a mob, heading for the Jewish quarter, shouting, stooping to pick up rocks, and accepting the knives and axes handed them by Thaddeus' hirelings.

In the ghetto the Jews heard the mob coming. They knew from past experience the futility of tryng to get help from the authorities. The men ran to their homes, yelling for their wives, hiding their children, and locking their doors in the desperate hope that the thin wood would stop the onslaught of raging men. By the time the mob hit the ghetto, there were hundreds, of them. They broke into the stores, carrying away valuables, destroying what they could not carry. Many forced their way into the houses, seeking gold, which rumor had it was hidden there. Others went looking for the beautiful women they had seen in the ghetto. A small knot of fanatics headed for the Synagogue "to avenge the wounds of Christ."

Pushing their way through the doors of the Synagogue, they rushed into the darkened sanctuary. Joseph Golem stood, as he usually did when he was not at work, near the Ark. In the darkened room, the fanatics were too excited to notice him. One of the men, an ex-seminary student, pointed to the Ark. "That's where they keep their devilish scrolls," he said. "Take them out and tear them to pieces!" Other voices chimed in, "Throw the scrolls into the gutter! Trample them!"

Rushing forward, the men opened the doors of the Ark. At that same moment, Rabbi Judah Loew came runing into the Synagogue. "Please don't touch them!" he cried out. "They are your Bible, too. Respect God's holy word!"

The men only laughed. One of them gave the rabbi a shove that sent him rolling across the floor, stunning him. Four men grabbed the four Torahs stored in the Ark. From the floor where he lay in a heap the rabbi cried weakly to the Golem. "Stop those men! Save the Torahs!"

The Golem stepped forward. With one hand he caught an intruder by the neck. The Golem's arm jerked. There was a loud crack. The others stood frozen as their comrade dropped at their feet. The Golem started for the second man who dropped his Torah and ran. The biggest of the group threw his Torah to one side and pulled a knife, advancing on the Golem slashing forward with the blade at each step. The Golem, easily avoiding the knife, reached down and seized the man by the waist, lifting him high above his head, and hurled him through the open Synagogue door into the street twenty feet away. At that, the fourth man fled for his life, the other fanatics close behind him, and the Golem pursuing.

Outside the Synagogue was complete chaos. Women ran screaming, chased by drunken peasants. Shouts, splintering wood, and cries of pain were everywhere. Acrid black smoke was begining to fill the narrow streets. Some looters had brought in carts in which to carry off valuables they had plundered. One of these carts was only a few feet from the Synagogue. The Golem smashed it with his fist; picking up two broken pieces of wood eight or nine feet long, he walked down the street, swinging these clubs, knocking down two or three men at a time.

Many peasants were too drunk to realize what was happening until the Golem loomed over them. Bodies flew right and left. Blood covered the streets. In less than half an hour, only the dead and wounded remained. Dozens of bodies were sprawled grotesquely in the gutters. Dozens of injured were trying to crawl away, leaving trails of blood.

The Golem marched all the way down the two principal streets of the ghetto and was on his way back when Rabbi Judah Loew managed painfully to climb to his feet and stagger out of the temple towards the Golem. The rabbi called loudly, "Golem, stop." The giant looked bewildered, hesitated a moment, them continued on, jabbing at whatever moved.

Rabbi Judah Loew felt a chill go up his spine. He perceived that the Golem was caught up in the joy of battle. The lump of clay which should have no emotions of its own, was acting as if human passions surged through its being. Perhaps his creation was developing a personality that would be beyond his control. He continued speaking, soothing the Golem with his voice and kind words until the giant calmed down, and finally obeyed his command to throw away the timbers and return to the synagogue.

In the streets there was quiet once again. Even the wounded and plundered realized that they had been saved from the mouth of death. A spontaneous feeling of joy swept through the community. People came to the synagogue to cheer the mute water carrier, the man who had saved them. After a few minutes of excitement, the rabbi called for quiet. He explained to his people that it was not proper to celebrate victory when wounded persons still needed care. "Those who attacked us, too, are the children of God," he said. He reminded them of the Rabbinic Commentary which tells how God rebuked the angels for celebrating when Egyptians drowned in the Sea of Reeds, saying, "Rejoice not over the downfall of your enemy."

The people of the ghetto began to help the wounded, friend and enemy alike. When that was done, they started repairing their houses and restoring to its proper owners, the property that lay about in the wagons and in the dirt of the streets. The next day, Yitzchok came to Rabbi Judah Loew and urged him to use the Golem at the head of a group of younger Jews to counterattack the gentiles. Surprised, the rabbi stared at Yitzchok and then sadly shook his head.

Yitzchok argued with him, speaking faster and faster, "Now is the time. Let the children of Israel see that their fathers are not at the mercy of the gentiles' evil whims. We should attack the barons and counts to teach them that Jews cannot always be beaten with impunity. We can loot their castles as they have looted our homes. And, perhaps, seeing us, the downtrodden gentile peasants will take courage and rise up against these aristocrats who exploit them. Now that God has given us this power, we should make use of it."

Rabbi Judah Loew refused, saying, "That is not our way. Our way is not with the fist, but with the book. Not with the sword, but with the word; with reason and with understanding; with Torah and with study." But Yitzchok went on arguing. He protested and urged long into the afternoon until finally Rabbi Judah Loew refused to say more on the subject, telling him it was time for evening prayers, and left.

Yitzchok was not convinced. Instead of going to say his prayers, he walked over to the Golem. He, too, had seen the enthusiasm with which the water carrier had fought. Yitzchok began talking to the Golem, telling him that he had helped in his creation and should be obeyed, too. When the

Golem failed to respond, Yitzchok added that he also knew the secrets of the Sefer Yetsirah and therefore, the Golem should follow him.

Still the Golem did not move. Yitzchok left the synagogue and returned with an ax. He held the ax out to the Golem. "We must destroy our enemies!" he said sternly. "Come with me." This time the Golem obeyed. Yitzchok led the Golem out of the ghetto. By this time it was dark, but Yitzchok knew the way to his destination. "We will destroy Thaddeus to start with," Yitzchok said. "He is the source of the evil which fell upon us."

As they came to the church where Thaddeus preached, Yitzchok thought, let us do unto them as they would have done unto us. He ordered the Golem inside, and pointing to the altar, shouted, "Cut down that altar! Smash their idols! Cut down the cross and chop it into bits!" The Golem lifted the ax. But before the blade came down, he remembered the words of Rabbi Judah Loew. Slowly and laboriously, the Golem began to think.

He remembered the rabbi crying out that the Torah was the Christians' Bible, too. He remembered the rabbi telling the people that the wounded gentiles were also the children of God. If that were true, how could he chop down this altar? The Golem turned and looked questioningly at Yitzchok. Yitzchok pushed at him in a frenzy of revenge, crying hoarsely, "Do it! Do it!"

Yitzchok grabbed the ax, swinging to strike the altar. The Golem caught hold of his arm, trying to restrain him, but Yitzchok fought wildly. The Golem tried to be gentle, but his strength was too great. He knocked Yitzchok down. Yitzchok rolled over and sprang to his feet, blindly attacking the Golem.

A kind of rage, the first of his brief existence, and as uncontrollable as a baby's, swept over the Golem. He twisted the ax from Yitzchok's hand and with one blow his fist bashed in Yitzchok's skull. Only a few minutes later, the rage left, leaving the giant looking down at Yitzchok's body in bewilderment and sorrow. He picked up the body and carried it back to the synagogue. Then he went to the rabbi's home and knocked on the door. As soon as Rabbi Judah Loew saw the Golem, he knew something was wrong.

Running to the synagogue, he found the body of his son-in-law. Even the great rabbi could not know exactly what had happened, but the memory of Yitzchok's words and the look of sadness on the Golem's face told him enough. The power he had created had corrupted his son-in-law. The young man had tried to misuse it and had met his destruction.

Yitzchok had been a good man, unswerving in devotion to God and the community. His flaw had been poor judgment in how to help his people and serve God. Shuddering at the thought of the destruction that would have taken place if Yitzchok had succeeded in using the power embodied in the Golem, Rabbi Loew concluded that what his son-in-law had attempted, others might as well. "Then, the responsibility for their actions would be mine, since I used my knowledge to build the Golem, and I know now the temptation he represents. The Golem is not an evil thing in himself, yet, for the people's sake, I must destroy him."

"Bend down," he ordered the Golem, intending to pluck from the giant's ear the bit of parchment inscribed with the vitalizing letters of God's highest name. But the Golem's mind was quickening. He perceived the reason behind the rabbi's request and shook his head. He had lived long enough to acquire an independent desire to survive, and would not willingly yield up his existence.

Rabbi Judah Loew stroked his beard, thinking wryly, the problems we make for ourselves can be as difficult as those that others make for us. I created this giant to solve one problem, but now my problem is how to destroy him. He measured the great height of the Golem with his eyes and shook his head. As long as the giant stood, it would be impossible to pull the parchment containing the true name of God—Yhvh—which was his life force, from his ear.

You may think that destroyng the Golem would not really be such a difficult problem for the great Rabbi Judah Loew who, after all, had the knowledge and power to create him originally from clay. Yet consider: Within our lifetime we have seen creations of less substantial stuff than clay—political parties, reform movements, revolutions—acquire a life of their own, and take over their own direction, resulting in actions beyond their creator's most frenzied intentions, and often end up by destroying those who began them.

Nevertheless, there are several different versions as to what happened, each one incorporating a different mystical insight into the nature of human-spawned creation, destruction, and power. I will relate a few of them. Do not, however, read them all on the same day, but read each ending on a different day. Follow your own intuition on which ending to read first. Then, when you have finished them all, wait one month and reread the entire account of the Golem with the ending you believe to be correct—not necessarily historically true, but spiritually correct.

I

But the Golem's mind was quickening, he perceived the reason behind the rabbi's request and shook his head.

"All right," Rabbi Judah Loew said. "I share the responsibility for what has happened for I created you. Come. Let us reason together. We will talk about what can be done." The Golem half turned as though to leave.

"Wait!" Rabbi Loew called out in alarm. "I know you are suspicious, Joseph Golem. That is an all too human characteristic. But I wonder if you have become human enough to be curious." Or, he added to himself, human enough to be ambitious and greedy? The Golem did not move, but his eyes cautiously studied the rabbi.

"I could reveal a secret to you," Rabbi Judah Loew said persuasively. "A secret about your creation which you could use to become even stronger and much more attractive. But if I do this for you, you must agree for your part to listen to my advice in the future before you act. If you agree to this bargain, lean down, and I will whisper the secret into your ear."

The Golem hesitated, obviously torn between desire and apprehension. Finally, with a look of cuning, he bent down in such a way that the ear lacking the parchment was inclined toward the rabbi, the other safely out of his reach. Rabbi Judah Loew began whispering. He whispered such marvels that the Golem's eyes opened wide in wonder and glazed. Softer and softer, the rabbi whispered; the Golem bent closer and closer, intent on hearing every word.

Suddenly with the quickness of a striking snake, the rabbi's hand darted out and grabbed the small bit of parchment from the giant's ear. Immediately, the Golem stiffened and toppled forward, crushing the rabbi under his weight. They died together, each one of them the victim of the other.

II

But the Golem's mind was quickening. He understood the reason behind the rabbi's request and shook his head. He turned and ran down the street faster than the rabbi could follow.Filled with despair, Rabbi Loew entered the synagogue and approached the holy Ark. Only a short time before, he had ordered the Golem to protect the Torah from destruction at the hands of the drunken mob of anti-Semites. But now he bowed his head and prayed for someone, something, to protect humanity from the Golem. All that night he remained in deep prayer. Finally, he became conscious that it was morning and that several people had entered the Synagogue and were waiting agitatedly for him to finish his prayers so that they could speak to him.

"Yes?" he said, straightening up.

"Rabbi, something strange has happened..."

"It's Joseph Golem, Rabbi..."

Still another troubled voice broke in, "Rabbi, you know Merle, Haim and Rifka's little girl? Well, Joseph Golem is holding her in his arms and he won't let her down. She is crying, but he just stands there without moving and we are afraid."

"Quick," said Rabbi Loew. "Lead me to them."

The men turned and ran out of the Synagogue, the rabbi following as fast as he could. When they reached the street where Haim and Rifka lived, he heard the little girl sobbing with fright and the Golem, standing at the top of some stairs, holding the child on his shoulder.

"He still hasn't moved," called out an onlooker. "Not a muscle."

Puzzled, the rabbi climbed the stairs and the little girl, seeing him, stopped her crying. But still the Golem did not move. The rabbi was about to speak when he noticed something in the child's hand.

It was the parchment with the name of God written on it. Apparently the Golem had picked up the little girl and placed her on his shoulder. Why? No one would ever know. But the child, noticing the bit of parchment in the Golem's ear, had playfully or curiously reached up and removed it. Without the mystical power of God's holy name to give him life force, the Golem became once more a rigid lump of clay. It had been only a happenstance, a fortunate one, that the giant's weight at that instant was perfectly balanced so that instead of crashing to the ground, injuring the child, he continued to stand erect like a statue.

The rabbi called to the child to let herself slide down the Golem's chest and he caught her, comforting her and taking the parchment from her hand as he set her down on the ground. Then he told the people, "Joseph Golem has died. We must honor him for the help he has given us," adding in his heart,. "It is not you who failed us, Joseph Golem, but we who are not yet ready for you."

III

But the Golem's mind was quickening. Perceiving the reason behind the rabbi's request, he shook his head, and Rabbi Judah Loew's heart filled with sympathy for this creature's wish to live. "All right," he said. "Let us submit ourselvels to the judgment of the Torah. Since you cannot speak, I shall argue your cause for you.

"In your defense, it can be said that Judaism does not teach pacifism. We believe a man has a right to defend himself. The Ten Commandments do not say, 'Thou shall not kill.' Kill is an incorrect translation of the word *Retsach*. It says, 'Thou shall not murder.' So it is not murder when a man kills in self-defense. You have a right to use violence to save yourself, just as the Jewish people have the right to protect and defend themselves against their attackers.

"On the other hand," said the rabbi, "when we fought the Roman Empire in the days of the Second Temple, and the Bar Kochoa rebellion, we did not succeed. The Rabbis have emphasized their belief that Israel shall survive by study, by spirituality, and by dedication to the mitsvot.

"And, indeed, we have survived fifteen hundred years since those days when we battled the Roman Empire. Although we have often been persecuted, massacred by the crusaders, victimized by pogroms during the time of the Black Plague, exiled from country after country in Europe, we have always survived. We have long outlived the Romans. We shall survive these medieval kingdoms which now harass us. They will tumble down, but the Jewish people will thrive. We survive not by force, but by the power of faith.

"On the other hand," said the rabbi, "a time may come when the gentiles may try to go further than their attempts on our faith; they may try to wipe out our very existence, our physical beings. Then shall we not defend ourselves? And will there not come a time during the battles of the Messianic Age when Israel shall once again, as in the days of David, have armies and generals?

"On the other hand," said the rabbi, deeply troubled, "could we not become corrupted even as Yitzchok was? Could we become like all the other nations, using our military power to persecute and exploit?"

There seemed no resolution to the problem. The arguments for were as strong as the arguments against. Rabbi Judah Loew began praying for a vision from God.

Suddenly he saw three and a half centuries into the future:

He saw his city of Prague; how changed it was in 1939 from the medieval town he knew. He recognized it only because his synagogue, the Altneu, still was standing. Then he saw the Germans marching into Prague. The city had fallen to madmen due to the pacifism of the French and the British, their unwillingness to fight the enemies of freedom, their willingness to buy peace for themselves in the conference room in Munich, at the price of lost freedom for others.

Rabbi Judah Loew saw his people rounded up and thrown into

concentration camps. He saw them persecuted and exiled in 1940 and 1941. He saw the Germans murdering men, women and children in the gas chambers in '42 and '43 and '44. He saw the British preventing the escaping refugees from reaching the land of Israel. He saw the Arabs misled into rejecting the homecoming of their Semitic brothers.

Then the rabbi began to cry. "I cannot destroy this Golem," he sobbed. "My people will have terrible need of him. But neither do I wish to have the responsibility for harnessing him now and using him against the anti-Semites. I will leave his use to a generation more desperate or much wiser than ours."

He persuaded the Golem to go up to the attic of the Altneu Synagogue and wait.

IIIa

He persuaded the Golem to go up to the attic of the Altneu Synagogue and wait. Some say Joseph Golem still was waiting for the Jewish people to call on him when the Altneu Synagogue was destroyed during the Second World War and that the Golem died, unused, in the flames of that destruction. They say the Jewish people had waited too long to become militant like the other nations.

However, it was whispered around Europe that when he was young, the founder and great leader of political Zionism, Theodore Herzl, ventured into the locked attic and discovered that the Golem had long since died and was as lifeless as an unbaked pot.

But as he stood, wide-eyed and sorrowing, looking at the inanimate form of the giant, Theodore Herzl, too, had a divine vision. He saw that the Golem could be brought to life again by the faith of the Jewish people. If the Jewish people worked together, and prayed together, and studied together, and fought side by side, they would regain their strength. A new state would be born, a fulfillment of the Messianic promise in the Torah.

The Jewish people themselves were a Golem waiting for the right spirit to bring them to life and strength.

Herzl's vision was right as history itself has verified.

IIIb

He persuaded the Golem to go up to the attic of the Altneu Synagogue and wait. During the Second World War, the Germans occupied Prague. Some of their officers had heard about the Golem, for the exploits of the Golem had been put on paper by Jacob Grimm, the famous German teller of stories. They went to the Altneu Synagogue with the intent of destroying the Golem along with all the Jews of Prague. When they broke down the attic door, they found the room was empty. There was only one spot in the dark room that was not covered by a thick layer of dust. Footprints led from that spot to the attic's window. The tracks could not have been made by a man; it was a giant's stride.

There have been many reports since then of the Golem. Some say he was present in Warsaw during the ghetto uprising. Others noticed him in the refugee boats, running the British blockade to reach sanctuary in the land of Israel. Men told of his power in battle during the Arab siege of Jerusalem, and in the battles in Galilee during Israel's War for Independence in 1948. Again in 1967 and 1973, the Golem fought in defense of the Jewish people. But one of his greatest battles will come in 1987, or 1997. Then he shall face the Russian bear and make it back down.

Those who fear that the Golem will corrupt the Jewish people and turn them into a nation like any other do not know the people of Israel. Even the Jewish army, impossible as its existence must have seemed a century ago, remains different from any other army. One need only study it to see the difference.

The Golem, too, and his spirit, which has been vitalized in this age of the birth pangs of the Messiah, prepares to revolutionize human conflict so that it may disappear at the conclusion of the Messianic Age.

After you have read the story of the Golem several times and decided which ending is true for you, you should realize that each ending represents a different perspective on the nature and use of power. Endings are, after all merely results. Every ending is simply a transitional stage to the next activity. Life always goes on. The results of our actions and beliefs are simultaneously endings and beginnings. The difficulty of living is that we make choices that are neither clear nor simple. They are not clear because we can not always see the outcome of our decisions. They are not simple because rarely do we choose between good and evil. Usually we choose the lesser of the two evils.

Because life's decisions are neither pure nor simple, we frequently not only suffer the consequences of our mistakes, but often add to that suffering by punishing ourselves for having failed to make the right choice. If we can only accept that a certain percentage of all decisions will be wrong for us as well as others, and still try and do the best we can, we can free ourselves of an unnecessary burden of regret.

Each of the endings to the myth of the Golem has much truth in it. The one that is right for you now may be wrong for you at a different stage in your life, or when you are in a different mood. Perhaps this is why truth does not consist of unchanging universals. Rather it is the total of several semi-contradictory insights, each appropriate in its own time and place.

I recommend the following books, all of which are well worth reading, each one selected for the ending that you chose.

First Ending: The Biblical Book of Ecclesiastes
Second Ending: I Never Saw Another Butterfly—Children's Poems
                 from a Concentration Camp
Third Ending: Tongue of the Prophet by Robert St. John
Fourth Ending: Man's Search for Meaning by Victor Frankel
Fifth Ending: The Sunflower by Simon Wiesenthal

MYSTERIOUS SOURCES OF THE KABBALAH

It is no coincidence that the origins of *mystery* and *mystic* can be traced back to the same Greek word meaning one who has been initiated into secret rites and, ultimately, to an even more ancient word meaning to close one's mouth.

It is the way of most Jewish mystics to keep their mouths closed about their inner visions. Some withdraw from normal society altogether. Even those who live among us are frequently indistinguishable from everybody else. They work, marry, raise children, laugh and cry, mingle with friends and keep secret the part of their life that is linked to God and the universe. Except perhaps for a disciple or two, the mystics' real nature is invisible to those around them, the important part of their life is mysterious, and their teachings are secret.

There are exceptions. Mystics like other people have differing personalities. From time to time a mystic comes along with a special dream, a feverish push, to hurry the coming of the Messiah by reaching out and lifting up great numbers of people all at once. These impatient mystics are the ones who make public the private teachings.

Over the centuries these revelations have dribbled out reluctantly, with anguish and soul searching. The reasons behind the tradition of secrecy are sound. Only a fierce inner urgency to hurry up the evolution of spirituality has persuaded some mystics to turn preacher and writer. But even when the decision was made, the habits of a lifetime do not drop away completely. Usually the revelations emerge shrouded in secrecy. More is kept back than made public. And as a result, almost as though the teachings were being protected, most people become so intrigued by the air of secrecy, they ignore the content of the revelation, to run after the mystery.

This is exactly what happened with the publication of the most important text in Jewish mystic tradition, the Sefer HaZohar (The Book of Splendor) or, as it is commonly called, the Zohar. The controversy that exploded with the Zohar's first appearance seven hundred years ago has not been softened by time. Rather, the quarreling has gathered force as the centuries pass and angry voices still rage among religious scholars and historians today.

Notice how events seemed to have conspired to keep attention away from the message of the Zohar, and focused on the manuscript's history.

The Zohar first was published in Spain sometime between the years 1280 and 1286 by a Kabbalist, Moses de Leon. De Leon claimed that the manuscript scroll had been found by Rabbi Moses ben Nakhman in a cave in the Land of Israel. Rabbi ben Nakhman sent the scroll by ship to his son in Catalonia, Spain. No sooner had the manuscript arrived in Catalonia than it was captured by a wind, or a spirit, and wafted to Aragon where it fell into his (de Leon's) hands. The true author of the scroll was the great sage and scholar, Rabbi Shimon ben Yohai. He had written the Zohar during the thirteen years that he and his son Eliezer hid from Roman soldiers after the failure of the Bar Kochba Revolt in the second century.

Now, Rabbi ben Nakhman, the one reputed by de Leon to have found the scroll, was himself a prestigious scholar. In fact, he was one of the most famous Rabbis of the thirteenth century.

His prestige so rankled established Christendom in Spain that the Dominican monks challenged him to a public debate. The Dominicans chose Pablo Christiani, feared among the intellectual jousters of Spain for his cold logic and slashing verbal attacks, to act as the champion of Christianity.

In an age when contests of debating were attended with all the passion and partisanship of a contemporary football game, it is not surprising that this major confrontation between the forces of Christianity and the forces of Judaism captured the imagination and interest of all Spain, and beyond to the whole of Europe. King Alfonso X attended the debate, which lasted several days, along with his royal ministers and a crowd of the realm's noted philosophers.

To the dismay of the Dominicans, who had expected to entertain the court to a spectacle of Judaism crushed, Rabbi Moses ben Nakhman presented the tenants of the Jewish faith with convincing clarity. King Alfonso was impressed. He expressed his admiration diplomatically: "I have never seen a man defend a wrong cause so well". Under cover of his words, he may have been impressed by the arguments as well as by Rabbi Nakhman's eloquence. Subsequent events suggest as much.

The king's diplomacy could not conceal the fact that Christianity was suffering a public intellectual humiliation. Outside the hall where the debate was being held, mobs of fanatic Christians were rioting in the streets. The Dominicans used this as an excuse to terminate the debate prematurely.

In those days religious freedom wasn't even an ideal, much less a reality. Even before the debate, the church in Spain had not eyed Rabbi Moses ben Nakhman with favor. After the debate, the eye yellowed with jaundice. Imagine then the reaction when Rabbi Moses ben Nakhman had the audacity to publish an account of the debate, spelling out the arguments that had captured the king's admiration, and caused the Dominicans to lose face.

Rabbi Moses ben Nakhman was called before a court in 1265, charged with blasphemy, and sentenced to be banished from the realm. The king tried to save him, delaying sentence while jealous churchmen fumed, to give the Rabbi time to complete the lengthy process of an appeal. However, the church in Spain went over the king's head, asking the Pope to intervene. In 1267 Pope Clement IV wrote a letter demanding that Alphonso punish the man who had "composed a tract full of falsehoods concerning his disputation with Pablo Christiani in the presence of the king, and even circulated copies of the book in order to disseminate his erring faith".

Rabbi Moses ben Nakhman left Spain, settling in Jerusalem in the fall of 1267. He died three years later.

If indeed he found the parchment manuscript of the Zohar and sent it to Spain as de Leon maintained, it must have been within those three years. Skeptics of de Leon's story wonder why Rabbi Moses ben Nakhman, who was engaged in writing his own Kabbalistic commentary on the Torah when he was in Jerusalem, would risk a lengthy and dangerous sea voyage for such a valuable scroll, rather than publish it along with his own manuscript in Jerusalem. Or, ignoring that issue, why the ten-to-fifteen year lapse between the time the scroll was said to have been sent to Spain, and its publication by de Leon?

At any rate, Rabbi Moses ben Nakhman had long been dead when the Zohar finally was published. He was beyond answering these questions either to verify or discredit de Leon's story.

One of de Leon's early skeptics was Rabbi Isaac ben Samuel, who in 1305 traveled from his home in the City of Acco, in the Land of Israel, to Spain to track down the Zohar's origins in person. The text had impressed him greatly, but certain sections seemed to him not to have been written by Shimon ben Yohai. His suspicions may have been awakened by the fact that the text had been written in two languages, Hebrew and Aramaic. Certainly, an author may be fluent in two languages, but usually a manuscript is written in only one.

After Isaac of Acco arrived in Spain, he began questioning all the Kabbalists he could find, about their knowledge of the Zohar's origin.

Some supported de Leon's story. Others maintained de Leon had written the book himself under the influence of a heavenly power. De Leon had ascribed the work to Shimon ben Yohai, they said, because he knew his copies of the work would bring a better price if it were supposed to have been written by a great sage rather than by an unknown spirit.

When at last Rabbi Isaac of Acco interviewed the man responsible for the controversy, de Leon insisted the Zohar came from an ancient manuscript in his possession. He invited Rabbi Isaac of Acco to accompany him to his house in Avila where the scroll was stored. There he could study it at his leisure and satisfy himself that the scroll was authentic.

Unfortunately, on the way to Avila, Moses de Leon took sick and died. It does not seem likely that de Leon died willfully to avoid being revealed as the perpetrator of a fraud. Nevertheless, his death had made it difficult, if not impossible, to solve the mystery with certainty.

Rabbi Isaac ben Samuel did not abandon his search for the scroll's author, exasperated as he may have been by de Leon's death. He continued on to Avila hoping to find the scroll among de Leon's effects. When he arrived he was told by a relative of de Leon that the ancient manuscript never existed. As evidence the relative pointed to the destitute state of de Leon's family. Not long ago, he told Rabbi Isaac, one of the community's wealthy men, Joseph by name, offered de Leon's widow a large sum of money and his pledge of marriage to de Leon's daughter, in return for the original manuscript. The mother and daughter replied sadly that the scroll had never existed. Moses de Leon had written the Zohar in his own hand, but to get a better price for his work, he ascribed it to the famous Rabbi ben Yohai.

In direct contradiction to this position, the Kabbalist Joseph ben Abulafia assured Isaac of Acco that de Leon really had owned the ancient scroll. Additionally, Rabbi Isaac met a disciple of de Leon who almost convinced him of the truth of de Leon's story. What the disciple said, we will never know. Maddeningly, the journal of Rabbi Isaac of Acco breaks off just at the point where he began to relate this testimony, and the missing section has never been found. Whatever it was, it failed to resolve all Rabbi Isaac's doubts. He is reported to have died wondering whether the Zohar had been written by Shimon ben Yohai or Moses de Leon.

The first surge of controversy died down, and within a century after its publication, the Zohar had assumed increasing importance in religious life. During the next few centuries hardly anyone doubted that the work had been written by Shimon ben Yohai.

However, skepticism of ben Yohai's authorship was reborn in the

eighteenth century. The challenges and disbelief grew louder and more vociferous during the next two hundred years.

By the nineteenth century, the Zohar had split Jewish scholarship into three warring camps. The loyalists stood by Shimon ben Yohai's authorship. The skeptics insisted that Moses de Leon had written the entire work. The third camp, manned by radicals with new ideas, applied the skills of the detective, the historian, and the linguist to the problem. They deduced from their studies that some parts of the Zohar could indeed have been written by Shimon ben Yohai, most of the book was the work of de Leon, while still other sections had been written by unknown authors at different periods of time. De Leon had possessed not only one manuscript, but several. How he came by them is a mystery, but they concluded, he had taken them and edited them, arranging the various sections as he saw fit and vastly expanding the material with his own writing.

Here are some of the most telling and interesting points in their reasoning:

1.   The Zohar uses a method of mystical interpretation of the Torah by the use of written vowels and accents as well as of consonants. This method effectively dates that section, because, the original scrolls of the Torah were written without vowels or accents. For centuries readers had automatically supplied the correct vowel sounds to written Hebrew from their own knowledge of how the word was pronounced. However, by the first century Hebrew ceased to be a spoken language. Thereafter, students learning to read the Torah were not sure how to pronounce the written words. A new system was invented in the sixth or seventh century of the present era, in which vowels and accents were written out along with the consonants. Obviously, Rabbi Shimon ben Yohai, who lived before the new system had been thought of, could not have used written accents and vowels to interpret the Torah.

2.   Another section of the Zohar refers to the custom of reciting Kol Nidray on the eve of Yom Kippur, a custom that began sometime in the ninth or tenth century, well after Rabbi Yohai's death.

3.   A description of a waterclock constructed to strike automatically at the hour of midnight, to rouse those who wish to be awakened for meditation, seems likely to have come from de Leon's time, inspired by the famous real-life invention of a waterclock by a Jewish scientist for King Alfonso X who ruled Castile from 1252 to 1284.

Although the authors of these passages in the Zohar are unknown, scholars do believe they understand how this later material came to be included in with the more ancient material.

Printing was invented smack in the middle of the fifteenth century, the first book off the press, the Guttenberg Bible, was believed to have been finished between 1450 and 1452. Before that time, books were handlettered, a long, laborious, boring process. Each book to be sold, each copy of a book to be made, had to be obtained in the same drudging way. Books were enormously expensive, largely due to the vast amount of time invested in each copy. A wealthy author could hire a scribe to do the copying for him. A poor man, and de Leon was certainly poor, must do the task himself.

Many of these handletterers, whether they were professional scribes, or authors, yielded to the temptation to add comments to the particular copies they were making at any given time. Additionally, teachers copying manuscripts for their students often included their own interpretations of the original author's meaning, or explained portions of the text through the use of contemporary illustration. Their students knew which passages were the original, and which their teacher's additions, and the manuscripts were handed down with great care from generation to generation. The long hours required to copy them made them far too valuable to use and discard. Three or four generations after the writing, readers would assume that the additions were part of the original text. And when that handwritten copy served as the model for making a new copy, the additions would be included in along with the original material.

Both customs were so common that scholars cannot assume all passages in any surviving ancient book are necessarily the work of the text's purported author. Copies were by no means the identical versions of a printed book we know today. In this particular case, not only had de Leon handwritten a number of copies of the Zohar, but many other handwritten copies of the Zohar had been made by the time it finally was set in print in 1558.

Although the waterclock incident may have been authored by de Leon or by an unknown scribe, the passages immediately preceding and following it, may well be letter perfect as Rabbi Shimon ben Yohai wrote them centuries before. Every sentence of every copy of a medieval handwritten book has to be checked for authenticity. More often than not, it is impossible to verify them one way or another. But like detectives who never give up on a case, scholars keep trying. It's the tantalizing frustration of unanswered questions that attracts minds of great intellect and greater curiosity to such text criticism.

4. Another suspicious section is the Ra'aya Meheimna which discusses the mystical significance of the mitzvot. It is known that Moses de Leon

had written several Kabbalistic books under his own name before the publication of the Zohar. One of them, a long treatise, the Sefer HaRimmon, was also on the mystical significance of the mitzvot. Curiously, the point of view of the Sefer HaRimmon is very different from the point of view of the Ra'aya Meheimna although they both deal with the same subject. This is not what you would expect if the same man authored both books. Further, the Ra'aya Meheimna actually refers to the Zohar, quoting from it, in several places. This suggests that the Ra'aya Meheimna was written some time after other sections of the Zohar, by a man who was familiar with the ancient text, but who was not de Leon.

In fact, the Zohar is not a single book at all, but like the Bible, a collection of many books. In modern editions the Zohar is usually divided into five volumes. The first three are customarily referred to as the Zohar on the Torah. The fourth volume is called Tikunay Hazohar (a commentary on the first few chapters of Genesis with digressions on grammer, prayer and Jewish law) and the fifth volume is the Zohar Hadash.

The last volume, the Zohar Hadash, is generally acknowledged to be a collection of saying from the fourteenth and fifteenth centuries which were found interspersed in later manuscripts of the Zohar and gathered together in the sixteenth century by the Kabbalists of Sefad, Israel who kept them with the rest of the text as an appendix.

The major part of the Zohar, the first three volumes, is arranged as a commentary on the weekly portion of the Torah. Traditionally, every Sabbath, members of a Jewish community gather together in their synagogue for a reading of the Torah. For that purpose, the Torah, the five Books of Moses, is divided into weekly portions which are read progressively each Sabbath over the lunar year of the Jewish calendar.

In its commentary, the Zohar is not noticeably zealous in sticking to its subject. Usually it interprets only a few verses in each weekly portion and then digresses to many subjects not related to the text of the Torah at all. (See "Divine Intercourse in the Zohar"). The Zohar's commentaries also interpret the Book of Ruth and the Song of Songs.

Several sections within the Zohar, the Idra Rabba (The Great Holy Assembly), the Idra Zuta (The Small Holy Assembly), the Midrash Ha-Ne'lam (the Hidden Midrash), and the Yanuka (The Infant or the Suckling) are more ancient than the rest. If de Leon did actually possess the original of a manuscript written by Rabbi Shimon ben Yohai, or a fragment of an ancient scroll by some unknown mystic, in all probability these were the sections it contained.

The discussion of the mystical significance of the mitzvot, titled the Ra'aya Meheimna (the Faithful Shepherd), which you remember probably was written by someone who had read the Idra Rabba, the Idra Zuta, and the Yanuka, is found as an independent work in some manuscripts. But more commonly, it comes broken up, each separate part placed in with the older section of the Zohar that comments on the same mitzvah. Most of the paragraphs from the Ra'aya Meheimna can be found in the Zohar's commentary on Numbers and Deuteronomy.

It is impossible, therefore, to date *the* Book of the Zohar because it is not one book but many. Like the Bible, sections of the Zohar were written under different conditions, in different times, by many different authors, each describing his own perception of mankind, existence, and the nature and destiny of Israel's mission in the world. Each section is valid and true within the conditions of its author's perception.

The first few chapters of Genesis show how divergent accounts of the same event can both be valid and useful because each views the subject through a different lens (See "The Secrets of Creation"). The scientific, universal account of creation presented in chapter one does not negate the validity or the importance of the psychological, existential account of man's evolution presented in chapters two and three. In the Zohar, you will find many examples of such seemingly direct contradictions, which actually represent complementary perspectives of reality.

No one knows who was the author of the Book of Job, or Ruth, or Samuel. Scholars are certain that David did not write all the Psalms attributed to him. It does not matter; the truth of a text does not depend in knowing the identity of the person who wrote it. What is important in a religious sense, is that it speaks to your heart, and makes you a more moral person.

Today we are obsessed by the personality of our authors. This development had its beginnings with the ancient Greek emphasis on the individual and the cult of personality. In the Jewish world, the author was considered not only less important than his writing, he was usually named after his work rather than the other way around.

In the Western world, we speak of Shakespeare's plays, or Kant's philosophy. In the Jewish world, the author would be known by his most famous work. Thus a Rabbi who wrote a text called "Tur" would be referred to not as Rabbi Jacob ben Asher but as the Tur. This, too, has psychological validity. After he died, those who knew him, knew him through the book. His personality lives on in the book. In the ultimate intellectual sense, to his readers, he is the book.

Whatever the facts behind the writing of the Zohar may have been, ascribing its authorship to Rabbi Shimon ben Yohai is charged with significance for the student of mysticism. Early rabbinic texts contain references to mystics and statements by them, but Shimon ben Yohai is never referred to as a mystic, nor is there a single mystical statement given in his name.

Now, Rabbi Shimon ben Yohai was a widely known scholar in medieval Europe. If he was a mystic, at first glance it seems strange that no hint of this appears in any of the texts which mention his name. Maddeningly, the absence of historical allusion to Rabbi Shimon ben Yohai's mysticism is cited both as evidence for and against his authorship of the Zohar. The obvious argument comes from those who say that his lack of contemporary reputation for mysticism indicates that he was not a mystic and, therefore, he could not have written a great mystical work. The more subtle argument points to the very absence of a prior reputation for mysticism as proof that no one would attribute the scroll's authorship to him, unless he actually was the author. The adherents of this argument point out that the Rabbi and his son, spent thirteen years hiding from the Romans. The effect of time and solitude in a remote mountain cave may have drawn them into mysticism. Then, after their return to the world, they may have decided to keep their mysticism secret.

This may be the hidden meaning of a story in the Talmud about Rabbi Shimon ben Yohai. When the father and son emerged from their cave after all those years of hiding, they found that life in their community was going on as it had before the attempted revolt. People continued to work in the fields. Boys and girls were holding hands, as though nothing had happened. The tragedy and suffering the Romans had inflicted on the nation, and on the two of them personally, apparently had been forgotten. The Talmud relates that Shimon ben Yohai became so enraged at this that wherever he looked, his gaze withered the plants and the trees, and killed all the life around him. At that point, a voice in the heavens was heard to say, "Have you come out only to destroy my world? If so, go back to your cave".

This story in the Talmud may not be taken from an actual historic event, but it may well hint that the Rabbi had become a mystic of such power that his presence threatened the stable existence of the Jewish community --- possibly by his example of total renunciation of wordly pursuits, or possibly by the danger that he might carelessly expose his mystical knowledge.

The Talmud seems to say that God gave Rabbi Shimon ben Yohai a choice: Learn to live in the world of mundane affairs and keep your mystical inclinations limited to those few who can profit from them, or return to the privacy of a cave, where your mysticism can hurt no one. But, of course, in the cave he would have been denied the opportunity to perform the mitzvot and so work for the redemption of the world.

He chose to remain in the world.

This seeming contradiction; that in the Talmud Shimon ben Yohai is never directly identified as a mystic, and yet the greatest text of the Kabbalah is attributed to him, may suggest to persons of understanding the dual goals of Kabbalists to pass along their mystical knowledge to the generations to come, while at the same time keeping secret their life as mystics.

There is no comparable debate about the second most important text in the Kabbalah, the Sefer Yetzirah (the Book of Creation). This is because we know nothing at all about its author.

The Sefer Yetzirah is amazingly short for an important text, containing less than two thousand words. It is rare in rabbinic literature because it contains only a few quotations from the Torah, and it is even more obscure in its meaning than the Zohar.

The Sefer Yetzirah was written in the Land of Israel, probably between the third and fifth centuries according to Professor Gershom Scholem, the greatest modern scholar of the Kabbalah. While the text has often been attributed to Rabbi Akiba, that claim only made its appearance in the thirteenth century. Earlier, it had been attributed to Abraham, the father of the Jewish people. Today, scholars are inclined to believe its author is, and will continue to be, unknown.

More than fifty commentaries have been written on the Sefer Yetzirah. Some of them are by the most famous Rabbis of the middle ages, including Rabbi Abraham Ibn Ezra, the great Biblical commentator; Rabbi Saadiah Gaon, the Head of the greatest Rabbinical School in Babylonia; and Issac the Blind, one of the most important innovators in the early Spanish Kabbalistic School. There is also a commentary on it by Rabbi Moses, ben Nakhman, who, according to de Leon, originally found the manuscript of the Zohar in the Land of Israel.

The Sefer Yetzirah is divided into six chapters, which in total contain only forty-seven short paragraphs. The opening two paragraphs refer to the thirty-two wonderful paths to wisdom. These are the Ten Sefirot and the twenty-two letters of the Hebrew alphabet, which were used in the creation of the universe. The Sefirot in the Sefer Yetzirah are not the same, however, as the standard description of them in the Zohar and the later Kabbalistic literature.

Most of the book is an attempt to interpret the nature of reality through the Sefirot, and the twenty-two letters of the Hebrew alphabet, in terms of science as it was known at that time. As our knowledge of science has developed considerably since the time of the Greeks and the Babylonians, there is little purpose in attempting to explain, or as is usually done, to justify the old science.

Rather, I will take Kabbalistic ideas and present them in terms of contemporary science (See "Intelligent Beings in Outer Space"). We understand that scientific theories always change as men acquire more data about the universe. In another century or two it will be necessary to reanalyze modern science as it will exist then, from a Kabbalistic point of view. Perceptions of reality do change with the changing generations of humanity, nevertheless, it is incumbent on each generation to attempt to understand the physical and metaphysical world in which it finds itself.

For me, the most important part of the Sefer Yetzirah is the opening two paragraphs. Most important of all is a single sentence which every commentator has realized is essential to the understanding of the entire book. That sentence consists of only three words: SFOR, SEFER, SIPPUR ‏ספור, ספר, סיפור‎.

Each of these words can be translated in several ways. Sfor means number or measure. Sefer refers to a scroll, a written text. Sippur means a story, a tale, a narrative. Each of these words can be read as a noun or as a verb depending on the vowels the reader places among the consonants. For that reason they can represent either actions or objects.

My interpretation of the statement is: There are three basic ways of understanding the nature of reality. First, there is the quantitative way, the method of science. Second, there is the academic way, learning from the history and culture of the community as a whole, through schooling and books. Finally, there is the method of personal experience, what some people call the school of hard knocks.

Each of these three methods is a path to truth.

The numerical or quantitative aspect of reality is closest to what we mean today by scientific truth. Truth or reality is what can be measured, weighed, and experimentally verified. The results of this method of understanding reality can be tested. It does not matter who does the testing, what his beliefs are, under what moral conditions the tests are made. So long as the physical conditions of the initial experiment are duplicated exactly, the results of the experiments will be the same.

In theory, the same is true in the field of logic, mathematics, or reason. Philosophers for centuries have believed they could find proofs which should be convincing to every person, because they were based on reason which is common to all. However, so many different schools of philosophy exist, because no philosopher has yet succeeded in finding such rational proofs. Mathematics comes the closest to being a universal truth. As a matter of fact, there are many who claim that the universe is, in its essence, basically mathematical. Time and again scientists have discovered some phenomenon of nature, and then realized that the phenomenon can best be described by mathematical formulae which had been developed out of pure theory, long before the physical discovery had been made.

Theoretical physicists and mathematicians are divided over this question; will all mathematics ultimately be found to correspond to every aspect of the real, observable, material universe? It does seem extraordinary that man's mind can discover, through mathematics, far in advance of observation, the nature of the physical universe. It is as though the Great Mind which planned this universe, had somehow given the small mind of man a reflection of the overall plan: mankind is in God's image, and mathematics is the image of God's design for the universe. From the Kabbalistic point of view, this is exactly what has happened.

The second path to truth and understanding is Sefer, the text. This is the way of civilization. It is the text that frees human minds from the monotonous chore of memorization. The great majority of the things we know, we do not discover for ourselves. Each generation accumulates knowledge and passes it on to the next generation primarily through the written word. If we had to rely only on the spoken word, and memorize all that we learned, as once humans did, society would be extremely limited in what it could pass on, and individuals would be even more limited in what they could achieve. Through the written word, people span distance and, even more important, they can span vast stretches of time. Thus, we read the thoughts of de Leon who lived in the thirteenth century as well as the unknown author of the Sefer Yetzirah who may have lived one thousand years earlier.

History is the record of humanity's development. It can teach us many lessons, and the Jewish people have shown themselves to be the most historical of all peoples. Jews have survived as a people for more than three thousand five hundred years. Of all cultures, civilizations, nations, or religions, that were in existence in the Western World at the time of Moses or David, the Jews alone continue as a cultural, religious and political entity.

The Kabbalah recognizes the written word as a method of transmitting the wisdom and insights from the past to the present and the future. The Kabbalah teaches us that writing is so important to man's development that it is sacred. The very letters of the alphabet have special powers and significance.

The third path to truth, is personal experience. Scientific thought is objective, easily verifiable to other investigators. History is not relivable or universal, but it is public. It recounts information to be shared by the community. But wisdom gained through one's life experiences is entirely personal and totally subjective. In some ways it is the most important wisdom of all because it is the wisdom that is true for you.

At the same time its importance is narrow because it is true for you only. The individual cannot successfully live in opposition to the wisdom of the community or objective scientific evidence. One may dislike the "law" of gravity, but if one decides to live his life in refutation of its principles, a painful fall is inevitable.

Science is limited to what it can measure: The world of "It". The community is limited to those experiences that are social and cultural, that relate to the external environment: The word of "We and they". You may read a book about love. You may make a scientific study of love. But the only way really to know love is to become a lover, to give yourself in love. The same is true for beauty, for faith, for religious experience, even for tasting an apple. Anything which involves feelings and perception must be experienced personally: The world of "I and thou".

Science is the perception of the rational, universal, objective mind. History is the perception of the community's mind. We relate to the social world around us, to the interaction between peoples and cultures. Personal experience comes from our own senses, our own soul.

It is important not to confuse the legitimate realm of each of these three approaches, Sfor, Sefer, and Sippur. To do so is to risk cynicism and materialism on one side, or fanaticism and escapism on the other. The risks of *inward* personal truth are illustrated in the Talmudic account of four great sages who entered deep into the grove of mystical speculation: Ben Azzai, Ben Zoma, Ben Abuya, and Akiba. Ben Azzai glanced within and died. Ben Zoma looked and lost his sanity; he had gone too far. Ben Abuya stared and lost his faith; he became a traitor to the Jewish people. Only Rabbi Akiba descended unharmed and ascended unharmed. Even though they were men of maturity, well versed in the Torah and Jewish lore, only one of the four survived unharmed.

Today with a blight of fake mystics and psychics offering instant enlightment, the casualties of mysticism will be even higher. *Only a personal insight which is supported by the Jewish community or the scientific community is safe.* Whoever takes the path of Sippur (personal insight) must make sure he or she is also supported by at least one of the other paths. To venture alone is to risk your health, your sanity or your soul.

Since Jews are committed to a monotheistic system, we must ask ourselves whether these three approaches to knowledge and wisdom do not ultimately become one. A profound and important teaching is that whenever you have three, there should be a fourth. Three is common in many mystical systems; it is a mystical number. But four is always truer than three. Knowing this, a student of the Kabbalah looks for a fourth path to wisdom, one that combines the other paths without blurring or obliterating their differences. Even a combination of any two paths would produce a worthwhile fourth, but the combination of all three into a fourth path would produce the most satisfying and effective method of all. Mystically it would be the purest and most powerful. Let it be your path!

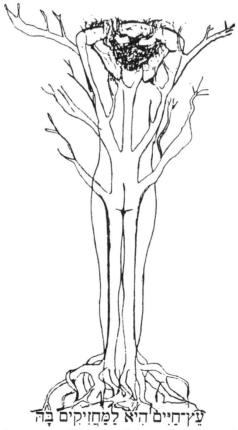

עֵץ־חַיִּים הִיא לַמַּחֲזִיקִים בָּהּ

She is a tree of life to those who grasp her,
And whoever holds on to her is happy.

THE HIDDEN CODE OF THE KABBALAH

How did God create the universe? By a thought? An idea? A mathematical equation? God used words. "And God said" appears ten times in the first account of creation. The ability to speak is unique to those created in God's image. In the Middle Ages when European scholars believed Hebrew was the language of creation, Hebrew was thought to be the original human tongue, the most ancient of all. We now know that this is not true. Several languages, such as Sumerian, are older than Hebrew, although Hebrew is the oldest living language.

Hebrew, the language in which the Bible was originally written, has one special aspect earlier languages lacked. It is written in alphabetical characters, instead of pictograms or glyphs, which required the scribe to make a picture of a house to indicate the word *house,* or of a man walking to indicate the word *walks.* To read glyphs or idograms one had to know thousands of different stylized forms.

The Chinese language still uses this method of notation. Its system is similar to the hieroglyphics of ancient Egypt, and over the centuries, it has acquired some fifty thousand different symbols standing for the words and concepts used in Chinese speech. A Chinese typewriter can have hundreds of keys; the machines are expensive and typing is cumbersome. To become literate in China, a person must memorize thousands and thousands of symbols rather than Hebrew's twenty-two symbols, or the twenty-six used in English.

Following the establishment of hieroglyphics, some cultures devised more sophisticated forms which represented the sounds of syllables as opposed to whole words. This improvement reduced the number of symbols needed to record the spoken language from thousands to only several dozen, but the process was still unwieldy.

The earliest known forms of writing go back six or seven thousand years. The development of phonetic symbols representing syllables occurred in several areas as independent inventions. But the alefbet (this is the Hebrew pronunciation) was invented only once in the history of mankind, sometime between the 16th and the 12th centuries before the common era, when in or near the land of Israel, a genius or a community of brilliant scholars, began using one symbol to represent a single, unchanging consonant sound. Once the relationship between each consonant sound and its unvarying notation is established, all the language's words can be written down by a reshuffling of two dozen symbols. The alefbet makes writing easy, encourages communication within the community, transmits culture to the young, and preserves the community's heritage for generations yet unborn.

The development of the alefbet was spread by the Phoenicians who lived just to the north of the Jews in what is now Lebanon. A seafaring people, they carried the alefbet and its use to the Greeks who pronounced the Hebrew letters alef, bet, gimmel, and dalid as alpha, beta, gamma, and delta. The Romans took the Greek alefbet, along with much of their culture, and passed it on to the European peoples they conquered.

The Hebrew alefbet is indeed the oldest of all alefbets and parent to all the rest. Kabbalists and many Christian mystics revere it, believing each of its 22 letters possesses a particular mystical power. For this reason most Kabbalistic meditation focuses on the forms of the Hebrew alefbet, rather than on silent chanting. Students can benefit from chanting a Hebrew word like שלום Shalom (peace) or אחד Ehod (oneness, unity), but visualizing the Hebrew letters of the word will greatly increase the effectiveness of the exercise.

To engage in Kabbalistic meditation, you should sit in a quiet place, blocking out all external sensory awareness, and focus your attention on the word you have chosen. When you can visualize the letters in different colors and watch them move in rhythm to your breathing, or see them as living flames — "the Lord is a devouring fire" you have readied yourself for a mystical experience. What word should you choose? Should it be שלום Shalom or אחד Ehod? The names of God are most propitious. And we Jews have a number of them, each connoting a slightly different perspective of God, or a different relationship to God. Choose the one that calls out to you.

There are the names for God found in the Torah, such as אל שדי El Shadai, so ancient that its use died out during the Biblical period, although it is still inscribed on the back of the parchment enclosed by the Mezuzah attached to the doorpost of a Jewish home. The most common Biblical name is אלהים Elohim, a pre Abrahamic term for the Divine. Grammatically, Elohim is plural, because prior to Jewish monotheism, the Divine was seen as many. Jewish patriarchs took the prevalent term, but, since they had learned that God was one, they used it with a singular verb form. Curiously enough, Christians point to this plural ending to support their belief in a Trinity; old beliefs die hard. Another Biblical name for God is יהוה צבאות Adonai Tsva'ot, the Lord of Hosts, implying the Divinity as a militant force or analogous to the power of team spirit.

The Talmud refers to God frequently as המקום Ha-Makom, the place, because the world is in place within Him, although He occupies no particular place in the world. A Talmudic expression of pious endearment for God is הקדוש ברוך הוא HaKadosh Baruch Hu, the Holy One, blessed be He. In mystical Judaism many names were constructed of much greater length than those used in daily prayers. The more complex names have 45, 52, and 63 letters, culminating in the famous name of 72 letters. These names were not meant to be used in conversation but served only as meditative exercises. The advantage was two-fold: The complexity of the name demands greater concentration, strengthening the mind and will, and the wealth of sacred letters in these names sanctifies the discipline and draws to it greater spiritual power.

The most powerful of all names for God is the name He gave Himself when Moses inquired who He was — יהוה YHVH.

I will have much more to say about YHVH later in this chapter. First we need to understand the code of the Hebrew alefbet. Early Kabbalists, such as the author of the *Sefer Yitzirah* thought the universe was created by mystical combinations of the 22 letters of the Hebrew alefbet. (Some scholars speculate that this theory was behind the selection of twenty-two as the number of cards used in the Tarot deck for telling fortunes.) However, the Kabbalists themselves, discovered a very different method of finding hidden meaning in life. This is Gematria, a code based on the numerical value of the Hebrew letters, but drawing its effectiveness from their mystical power.

Gematria was used and is still being used, to uncover the Torah's hidden meanings and its prophecies, and to obtain guidance for personal insight. The use of special symbols to designate numbers is relatively modern. Ancient languages such as Hebrew, Greek, and Latin, used the letters of their alefbet to indicate numbers. Hebrew assigns to the first letter (alef) the value one, the next letter (bet) the value two, etc. Every written word in Hebrew has a numerical value, the sum of its letters. To illustrate the process in English, the word Bad can be thought of a 2(b) + 1(a) + 4(d) = 7(G).

Central to the Gematria's system is the idea that two words with the same numerical value have a mystical relationship. The numerical sum of the Hebrew word משיח *Messiah* (the anointed one) is 358, the same value as the Hebrew word נחש *Nachash.* Knowing this equivalence is a key to understanding the role of the serpent in the Garden of Eden as God's agent for bringing about humanity's enlightenment (see "Secrets of Creation"). Another simple Gematria provides insight into the nature of love. The numerical equivalent of אהבה ah-ha-vah is 13. One "love" added to another — two lovers — equals 26. And 26 is the Gematria for יהוה YHVH, the true name of God. Thus, two people in love participate in a Divine experience.

Here is a Gematria which has meaning for our own time. The Book of Ezekiel (chapters 38 and 39) predicts the appearance in the future of a major enemy, named גוג *Gog,* who will arise and try to destroy the Jews. The Gematria for *Gog* is 12. During the Talmudic period, the rabbis applied the name ארמילוס *Armilus* to the major enemy of Israel, who would, in the end of days, try to destroy the Jewish people. (*Armilus* was used as a disguised reference to Rome, supposedly founded by Romulus.) The Gematria for *Armilus* is 347. If we symbolically combine the characteristics of ארמילוס *Armilus* and גוג *Gog* by adding their separate sums, we have a Gematria of 359. This Gematria exactly equals the numerical value of שטן Satan. Now, if we add the numerical equivalents for the Hebrew letters for the name אדלף הטלר Adolph Hitler, we get exactly 359. Thus, the Gematria tells us that Adolph Hitler was *Gog* and *Armilus* combined, Satan, the embodiment of mankind's malice as it is focused on an effort to destroy God's Chosen People (for more details see "The Coming of the Messianic Age").

The Gematria for Messiah is 358, while the Gematria for Jesus-Yeshua- is 386, not equivalent as it would be if he had been the true Messiah. No Hebrew name for God has a Gematria equaling 386, Jesus' Gematria, nor do they equal the 28 points that separate Jesus from Messiah. The name of God that is closest in value to the 28 point difference is YHVH. The Gematria of YHVH is 26, 2 short of 28. Some Jews have said that Jesus was a false, deceiving Messiah, but the Hebrew word *Kezev* כזב, which means liar or deceiver, has a Gematria of 29, one more than 28. Thus, examination by Gematria tells us that Yeshua was neither Divine, nor a false prophet, but somewhere in between. He was, in fact, a Messianic figure who failed.

Here is an example of the use of a Gematria as a guide to daily living that has proved helpful to me. The Gematria for צחוק *tzhok* — laughter — is 204, the same value as the Gematria for נצחון *nee-tza-hon* — victory. This equivalence teaches us that if we can only laugh at life's frustrating situations, we can achieve victory over them. It also teaches us that unless

GEMATRIOT

דיבוק = 122	Dibook		אהיה אשר אהיה = 543	I will be what I can be
גילגול = 82	Gilgul		תורה = 611	Torah
גֵיהִנוֹם = 114	Gehenom		אחרית הימים = 724	The end of days
גן עדן = 177	Gan Eden		אדם הראשון = 607	The primal human
אדם = 45	Adam		אדם הקדמון = 250	Arche type human
חוה = 19	Eve		מטרוניתא = 716	Kabbalistic name
נחש = 358	Nahash			for the Shekenah
משיח = 358	Messiah		ברית עולם = 758	Eternal covenant
יהוה = 26	YHVH		נחמיה בן חושיאל = 520	A name of the Messiah
אלהים = 86	God		שער שמים = 960	Heavenly gate
שְׁכִינָה = 385	Shekenah		פני שבת = 842	Sabbath presence
צִימְצוּם = 276	Tsimtsum		משיח בן דוד = 424	Messiah son of David
לילית = 480	Lilith		משיח בן יוסף = 566	Messiah son of Joseph
שטן = 359	Satan		אריך דאנפין = 426	Kabbalistic name
תיקון = 566	Tikun			of God
חבלי המשיח = 408	Hevley Hamoshe'ah		שמע = 410	Shma
אין סוף = 207	Ain Sof		שלום = 376	Shalom
עץ חיים = 228	Ets Hayim		אֵל שדי = 345	El Shadai
בית האלהים = 498	Bet Haelohim		מצוות = 542	Mitsvot
פני משיח = 498	Pnai Moshe'ah		גולם = 79	Golem
ישראל = 541	Israel		אחד = 13	One
שופר = 586	Shofar		אהבה = 13	Love
ירושלים = 596	Jerusalem		אהיה = 21	God of Becomming
אלהי ישראל = 587	God of Israel		הקץ = 195	The End

Alef Bet = Numbers

א =	1	ל =	30
ב =	2	מ =	40
ג =	3	נ =	50
ד =	4	ס =	60
ה =	5	ע =	70
ו =	6	פ =	80
ז =	7	צ =	90
ח =	8	ק =	100
ט =	9	ר =	200
י =	10	ש =	300
כ =	20	ת =	400

we enjoy our minor successes with a child's laughter of delight, they do not become the victories they should be. Thus, laughter — *tzhok* — leads to victory, and victory — *nee-tza-hon* — should lead to laughter.

By now it must be clear that learning Hebrew is essential to mastering the Kabbalah and using Gematria. Fortunately, the language is easy to learn. Its alefbet is phonetic so that once you have learned the sounds of its 22 consonants and its more recently developed vowel signs, you will already be able to read Hebrew writing. Memorizing enough of the vocabulary to understand what you have read is another matter. However, it is not necessary to know a prayer's meaning, word by word, in order to chant it. Most mystics believe that prayer which comes from the heart imparts non-rational communication and is the truest way to dialogue with God.

Hassidic Jews tell a story of a young orphan boy, coming to the synagogue to pray on Yom Kippur, the holiest day of the year. While the congregation reads the prayers, the little boy stood speechless because he didn't know how to pronounce the letters written in the prayer book. All he could remember from his few months of Hebrew school was reciting the alefbet. So, he began saying the alefbet over and over, hoping that, as it was the only thing he had to offer, God would take the letters and arrange them to make an appropriate prayer. When Yom Kippur ended, the rabbi told his congregation, "All of your prayers were weighed down with routine and half-heartedness. They wouldn't have risen if it weren't for the prayer of one little boy whose fervor carried them all the way to the heavenly throne".

An example of a Kabbalistic prayer that involves code technique follows. You will note that it can be read in all four directions. Recite it continuously for 5 minutes in a fixed pattern of movement. Then close your eyes, picture it, and do it for 15 minutes entirely in your mind. The more complicated the pattern of directions the better.

Please	Sire,	grant	desire,	forgive	error,	banish	terror
Sire	please,	desire	grant,	error	forgive,	terror	banish
Grant	desire,	forgive	error,	banish	terror,	please	Sire
Desire	grant,	error	forgive,	terror	banish,	Sire	please
Forgive	error,	banish	terror,	please	Sire,	grant	desire
Error	forgive,	terror	banish,	Sire	please,	desire	grant
Banish	terror,	please	Sire,	grant	desire,	forgive	error
Terror	banish,	Sire	please,	desire	grant,	error	forgive.

Until you have learned enough Hebrew to use Gematria to discover the meditations and mitzvot especially propitious for your own spiritual development, you can use this system to guide your studies. Take the Book of Deuteronomy and read from chapter twelve to chapter twenty-six, paying careful attention to those verses which have the same number as the month or day on which you were born. Also pay attention to the verses whose number is equal to your age, and the age of the person you love most. Do not merely look at these verses out of context jumping from chapter to chapter, but read slowly and thoughtfully with an open mind and heart.

The simplest and yet most profound code word in the Torah is the name of God, YHVH. God is one; God's names are many. Each name, Buddha, Krishna, Jesus, Allah, represents a different religious view of the Divine One. Each perspective shapes different philosophic and psychological characteristics in its followers. Usually once the shaping has been accomplished, it is best to stay within the disciplines of that perspective because they touch you at your heart's core. Switching around from discipline to discipline may make us intellectually glib, but it rarely brings us close to God. That comes from constancy, diligence, and desire.

With God it is better to know one name thoroughly, than to dabble among a dozen. After all, if we know a hundred of His names, there would be hundreds more yet to learn. No human being can master the infinite perspectives of the Divine One.

For those of us living in great urban areas where we meet and become friends with people worshipping God with different names and different disciplines from ours, it is important to remember that the various perspectives of the Divine One can be contradictory without being in error. No religion can claim its view of God is the only true one. It is enough to love our view of God. That experience should help us appreciate the experience of another who loves a different view of God. The view is not the same, but the love is similar, and God is One.

How did the different religions come by their different names for God and their different rituals of worship? Often by revelation. Then why do they differ so much? Let us look at a great example of Divine revelation at work, in the Book of Exodus, chapter three. One day while Moses was herding sheep for his father-in-law, he saw a bush in flames and walked over to the bush to see what was happening. When God saw that He had attracted Moses' attention, He called out to Moses.

Moses took advantage of God's opportunity. Others might have been too engrossed doing their job of keeping the sheep together to take the time to study a burning bush. Or if they saw the flames, they would simply shrug their shoulders over some freak of nature. They would not think it was a marvel; they would not let themselves perceive a miracle. We often overlook the marvels in the world about us. We take for granted the wonder of being alive and being part of God's creation. We take love for granted, and friendship, and all the extraordinary relationships we have with the world about us. We miss the miracles in our lives. And, so, God does not speak to us. He did not call out to Moses until Moses had turned aside to examine the burning bush, because if Moses was blind to the miracle of the bush, he would be deaf to the voice of God.

If someone had been on the spot with a tape recorder those thousands of years ago, would he have been able to record the voice of God calling to Moses? Of course not. God has no body, and therefore, no audible voice. When the Divine speaks, it is not an externalized call, but an internal feeling. Some naive people believe you have had a real experience if your ear picks up vibrations coming through the air and sends nerve impulses to the brain; but you have had a hallucination if your mind receives the communication directly, without the intervening media of air, ear, and nerves. This is prejudice, not logic. The feeling of being loved is just as tangible as hearing the words, "I love you." The inner perception of truth is no less reliable than the perception of truth through the senses of sight and sound. It may be more reliable. How often has someone lied to you? Perhaps, more often than you have lied to yourself.

Moses heard the voice of God, telling him to go to Pharoah and lead the Jewish people out of bondage in Egypt into the Land of Israel. Understandably, Moses felt overwhelmed by the task. More important to us, he asked, "When I come, who shall I say sent me?" Remember, Moses was hearing a disembodied voice. He was really asking, "Who are you?" God answered, אהיה אשר אהיה "Aheyeh asher Aheyeh", revealing both his name and his nature. He told Moses, "Thus shall you say to the Children of Israel, אהיה 'Aheyeh sent me to you'. This is my eternal name, to be used throughout all generations." (Exodus 3:14)

In referring to Himself, God used the first person of the Hebrew verb to be, in the future tense, Aheyeh, but when we refer to Him we use the third person future of the verb to be, YHVH in its causative form meaning He who will bring into being. YHVH is usually mispronounced Jehovah or Yahweh. Only Moses knew directly from God how His name should be pronounced. Moses did not pronounce God's name to the community. He whispered it only to a few who were strong and holy enough to withstand its inherent power. According to some teachers, only two people in each generation know the sound of God's name; and on their deathbeds, those who know whisper the true pronunciation of God's name to the most devoted, diligent, and reliable of their students.

When the Torah was being written down, God's true name was recorded, but not the pronunciation. Originally, the entire Bible was written without symbols for the vowel sounds. The vowels were not added until the late Roman, early Moslem period when Hebrew had long since ceased to be a spoken language; and including written symbols for the vowels was necessary to help people pronounce the words.

The true name of God like the presence of God, cannot be safely confronted by most of us. Our inability to say God's name reminds us that God is the אין סוף Ein Sof; the infinite, the unbounded, the unlimited, the indefinable. The Ten Commandments forbid us to make an image of the Divine because an image of God resembling something in the heavens above, or on the earth, or in the ocean beneath the earth, is a kind of sacrilege. It cannot be a true representation. A name is more abstract than an image, yet even that too, can become a definition, thus limiting the Infinite One. Remember Moses did not hear God's voice in his ears; he felt it his heart.

Most religions do symbolize their perspective of God in concrete forms, using statues and pictures. But Jews remind themselves, by the absence of imagery, and by even avoiding the pronunciation of God's name, that God cannot be contained in a symbol, that the reality of God is forever beyond us. More often than not Jews refer to God by saying אדוני *Adonai* — Lord, just as the usual translation of YHVH in English versions of the Bible is Lord. It would be better, however, coming upon this word YHVH simply to pause, to verbalize nothing, to imagine nothing, to feel the silence. Then, perhaps, in our innermost souls we would learn a little of the unknowable nature of the Infinite, the Ein Sof.

Moses asked, "Who shall I say sent me?" And God answered, *"Aheyeh asher Aheyeh".* The usual translations of His reply are inadequate. The most common, "I am that I am" is not only inadequate, it is false, because the verb is clearly future tense, and it conveys a false impression of the Deity.

Translating God's reply into the present tense implies that God is, and always will be as he is now. This translation suggests that God is the perfect, unchanging, all-powerful, all-wise, self-sufficient God postulated by the ancient Greek philosophers. But that is not true! If God was all-knowing, He would know the future, robbing humanity of free will. Similarly, if He was all-powerful, there could be no wrongdoing in the world since God Himself is good. In order to give humanity the opportunity to discover right from wrong, and the freedom to choose evil actions or good actions, God must have limited Himself. He withdrew His capacity to be all-powerful and all-knowing in order to give us moral knowledge and the power of moral action. (see "Intelligent Life in Outer Space").

In Hebrew the future tense of the verb *to be* may be translated as I will be, or I may be, or I could be. This flexibility of meaning conveys information about God's relationship to us: God is open to change and evolution in the future. The meaning "I will be what I will be" is a promise that He is the essence of limitless potentialities; He will be whatever His people need Him to be. "I could be what I will be", or "I could be what I may be", implies that God's future depends on man's future; as humanity evolves so will our concept of God evolve and so will our relationship to God. Since YHVH is based on the Hebrew verb *to be,* we may infer that God is being. God has been called Absolute Being, but this is a static concept. From the Kabbalistic perspective, the important tense is the causative one. YHVH is causative: God is He who causes to be; God is the essence of what should be or what might be, the potentiality of the future.

The Divine dimension is not space, as those who make images and pictures imply. Time is the Divine dimension. The whole universe is permeated by time flowing in one direction, from the past through the present toward the future. The universe evolves in such a way that nothing can be repeated exactly as it was before. Nothing is permanent under the sun. Everything changes. A true understanding of the nature of God helps us meet the changes in our own lives, without clinging to the past in dread of the unknown, confident that God will be with us. Future change is possible only because He is present now. The Divine dimension is the potentiality for development. It contains the promise that humans can achieve the potential implied by their having been created in the image of God. It is the guarantee of our faith in the Messianic achievement.

SEX AND DIVINE INTERCOURSE
IN THE ZOHAR

The concept that sex is holy startles most people in the twentieth century because western society has recoiled from puritanical suppression of sex, to pornographic sexual exploitation; and either approach degrades sex. Our generation is badly in need of the Zohar's insights into sexual holiness. Therefore, although the Zohar is not primarily concerned with the metaphysics of sexual relationships, I have selected several passages from its text to answer this particular need. These passages, which are among the less difficult and esoteric in the Zohar, will serve the purpose of being an introduction to the Zohar's method of teaching.

The Zohar is the most important of all the Kabbalistic works. *Unfortunately, most English books on Kabbalah fail to present more than a few short quotations from the actual text, and then try to arrange the Zohar's ideas in a systematic order. But, the Zohar's ideas do not come to us systematically in the original text. They emerge as commentaries on the holy Torah.* The author of the Zohar follows the tradition of most Kabbalistic and Rabbinic works. His ideas are responses to Torah ideas, and at times he becomes excited by a divergent thought and digresses.

This approach to teaching conforms more closely to the way we learn from living than the usual classroom or textbook experience. Life is not logical or systematically organized. Neither is Jewish religious thought. Most Jewish religious thought is not presented in a logical and systematically organized way, because life just isn't like that. Insights are achieved here and there, and at times they even contradict each other. Truth resides not in the artificial reconciliation of variety, but in the realization that truth is manifold.

Traditionally, even advanced students of the Kabbalah use a commentary to study it. Any novice who claims to understand the Zohar without the help of a teacher or a commentary suffers from illusion. This chapter contains several pages selected from the Zohar itself. It also includes my commentary. I have tried to follow the Zohar's teaching method in my commentary, allowing my intuition rather than my sense of logic to guide me. I hope my intuition touches yours. Read the selections first to get a feel for the original text. Then after reading the commentary, reread the text. The second time around should be an entirely new experience.

Don't be discouraged if the going is difficult. Remember that obscurity is at the heart of the Zohar's method. Take a chance the method will awaken your spirituality. The insights of the Zohar emerge slowly and gradually as you study. My commentaries represent only what I have understood to date.

In the Western world the writer is expected to explain everything clearly and systematically to the reader who is expected to be passive. In fact, part of the respect we give a book is based on our knowledge of its author and his accomplishments. The Jewish literary tradition is different. The ultimate author, in the highest sense, is the Holy One, Blessed is He. Most authors see themselves as commentators who merely deepen the insight and enrich the understanding of the basic revelations which appear in the Torah.

Since the Torah was revealed to the whole Jewish people, every Jew was expected to study, and if possible add to the understanding of Torah. Thus a Jewish reader is expected to dialogue with the text, seeing the problems, the complications, the ambiguities that exist, and evaluating the commentator's attempts to deal with them. In fact, there is usually more than one commentary printed on each page of a volume of the Bible or the Talmud. Often there are more than half a dozen commentators arguing among themselves. I have purposefully not commented on every line or concept in the selection that you will read in order to leave you room to test your own wits. The Commentary, following the form of a traditional commentary, is sometimes precise and sometimes verbose. Digressions are included for, as in the case of the Talmud, a free association of ideas frequently leads one astray to greener pastures.

The mixture of modern statistics with ancient concepts is the author's contribution to the tradition of his ancestors. Now try to understand the Zohar's teachings on Divine intercourse.

"Adam and Eve, as we have said, were created side by side. *Why not face to face?* For the reason that heaven and earth were not yet in complete harmony, 'The Lord God had not caused it to rain upon the earth' (Gen. 2:5). When the Lower Union was

"Why not face to face?" This seems an obvious question. However, very few people know that in the entire world there are only four other animals that have intercourse face to face. They are the two toed sloth, the

rendered perfect, and *Adam and Eve turned face to face,* then was *the Upper Union perfected.*

"This we may know from the matter of the tabernacle: for we have learned that together with it there was put up another

pygmy chimpanzee, the hamster, and the porcupine, the latter for reasons that should be obvious.

Man, however, is the only animal capable of having sexual intercourse in more than one position. This is part of our divinity, for it makes human sex supernatural. That is to say, human sex unlike animal sex is not simply a natural means of reproducing the species. Our sexual behavior, and the feelings which precede and flow from sexual interaction, are based on our culture's religious values, and on our own unique personalities. Mankind is the only animal who engages in sexual intercourse for purposes unrelated to procreation, i.e., for purposes of recreation, or love. The variety of human positions in sexual intercourse is of no value for procreation purposes. But it does have spiritual value for increasing the duration and intensity of human sexuality. This additional factor, which indicates man's superiority to the animal world, is part of humanity's link with the divine.

"Adam and Eve turned face to face." You might think that this is the only proper position. Many people have a revulsion for any position other than the usual one of the man on top and the woman underneath. The Talmud records several opinions stating the negative effects of alternative positions. In tractate Kallah we find the following statements: "if one has intercourse sitting, he will be subject to diarrhea. If he is below and she is above, he will be seized with convulsions." Another statement: "If one has intercourse when drunk, his heart will ultimately be affected. If both of them are drunk, their hearts will be affected." Rabbi Yohanan Ben Dahabai says that the ministering angels told him children are born dumb because their parents kiss each other's genitals.

In spite of the fact that various rabbis have particular practices that they were opposed to, and that Rabbi Yohanan even claims he got his information directly from the angels, the Talmud concludes the discussion as follows: "the sages say that the Halakah (The Law) is not in agreement with Rabbi Yohanan Ben Dahabai, but a man may do with his wife as they desire because the matter can best be compared to someone who purchases meat from the butcher; if he wishes, he eats it roasted; if he wishes he eats it salted. Or to someone who has purchased fish from a fisherman; if he tabernacle, nor was the upper one raised until the lower one was erected: and so it was in this case. Moreover, inasmuch as all above was not yet perfectly ordered, Adam and Eve were not created face to face.This is borne out by the order of the verses in scripture: first it is written, 'For the Lord God had caused it to

wishes he eats it salted; if he wishes he eats it roasted; if he wishes he eats it grilled over coals."

In other words, it is all a matter of taste. There is no right or wrong way to prepare food. Individuals differ considerably in their appreciation of different types of food and we are all better off because we are able to choose a variety of different styles of food, i.e., Chinese, Italian, Jewish, Japanese, French, etc. So, too, in the matter of fulfilling sexual relations, anything that both parties find appetizing and desirable, and which neither finds distasteful or embarrasing, is to be considered Kosher... fit, suitable, okay.

"The Upper Union perfected." Sexual intercourse between husband and wife can be the highest perfection in the world of nature. In truth it is a state in which nature is transcended in spirituality and ecstasy. Sex, then, can be supernatural and divine. The Jewish idea that the sexual relationship between a husband and wife is holy, a Mitsvah, is opposite to Greek philosophy which strongly influenced Paul, the founder of Christianity. He wrote, "It is good for a man not to touch a woman." (Corinthians 7:1). Of course he realized that if his disciples really followed his teaching, the newly organized Christian church would only last one generation.

In addition, he must have realized that very few Christians would really keep celibate, and not having their own husband or wife, they would go after someone else's. So he immediately added "Nevertheless, to avoid fornication, let every man have his own wife and let every woman have her own husband." Yet in his heart, he would have preferred that "all men were even as I myself." Paul never married; neither did Jesus. So Paul advises, "I say therefore to the unmarried and widows, it is good for them if they abide even as I. But if they cannot contain themselves, let them marry; for it is better to marry than to burn. And unto the married I command, (not I, but the Lord) let not the wife depart from her husband. But if she depart, let her remain unmarried:" (Corinthians 7:7-11).

Of course, very few Christians follow Paul's teaching. Priests and nuns do, and the Catholic Church retains its ban against divorce, but the rain upon the earth,' and following, 'There was not a man to till the ground,' and it signifies that man was yet imperfect, *for only when Eve was made perfect, was he then made perfect too.'*(Zohar Genesis 34a).

majority of Christians ignore or reject these Christian principles as being unrealistic. From the Jewish point of view they are not just unrealistic, they are wrong. They are sinful and depraved. Marriage is a Mitsvah and so is sex. It is strange that Paul who was so down on sex was at the same time so much in love with love. This is how he speaks of love: "Love is long suffering and kind; love envieth not; is not proud or puffed up; it does not behave in an unseemly way, is not easily provoked, and does not think of evil. Love bears all things, believes all things, hopes all things, endures all things; love never fails. (Corinthians 13:4-8).

It is clear that Paul's ideal of love dosen't really exist. What human lover embodies all those virtues? By developing a dichotomy between the ideal of love on one hand, and the baseness of sex on the other hand, Paul and the Church perverted the natural harmony of spirit and body which is so beautifully contained in divine intercourse. Paul could not conceive of marriage as being a Mitsvah. At best, he conceded, "if thou marry, thou hast not sinned; and if a virgin marry, she hath not sinned. Nevertheless such shall have trouble in the flesh." (Corinthians 7:28).

"For only when Eve was made perfect was he then made perfect too." It is Eve who makes Adam perfect. This refers, as we have described in the chapter on the secrets of Creation, to the fact that Eve ate of the fruit of moral knowledge first, thus becoming morally aware and so capable of perfection like God. Then she gave the fruit to Adam who also ate and become like God, knowing good from evil. Thus again we see that it is woman who makes man perfect and not the other way around.

The Zohar to Genesis (49b) teaches explicitly the divine nature of intercourse. The passage is as follows:

"Remark this. The whole time of his traveling a man should heed well his actions, lest the holy union break off and he be left imperfect, deprived of the union with the female. If it was needful when he and his wife were together, how much greater the need when the heavenly mate is with him? And the more so, indeed, since this heavenly union acts as his constant guard on his journey, until his return home. Moreover, *it is his duty*, once back home, *to give his wife pleasure*, inasmuch as she it was who obtained for him the heavenly union.

"There is a twofold reason for this duty of cohabitation. First this pleasure is a religious one, giving joy also to the divine

"It is his duty." According to the Torah and to Rabbinic law, a husband is expected to provide his wife with food, clothing, and sex. (Exodus 21:10). The rabbis discuss the question of how often a man should make love to his wife in order to fulfill this Mitsvah. They decided that it depends on his health and his occupation. Those who are in leisurely professions, who have wealth, or do not have to be concerned with making a living, should make love every day. For the average worker, it should be twice a week. (The famous Kinsey report on sexual behavior in the United States indicated that the average couple did have sexual relations about twice a week.) For those who are engaged as traveling salesmen or on other jobs that keep them away from home, the Mitsvah should be fulfilled at least once a week. Rabbi Moses Maimonides, the great twelfth century philosopher and legal expert, wrote in his code of Jewish law as follows: "The conjugal rights mentioned in the Torah are obligatory upon each man according to his physical powers and his occupation.

"How so? For men who are healthy and live in comfortable and pleasurable circumstances, without having to perform work that would weaken their strength, and do nought but eat and drink and sit idly in their houses, the conjugal schedule is every night. For laborers, such as tailors, weavers, masons, and the like, their conjugal schedule is twice a week if their work is in the same city, and once a week if their work is in another city.

"For ass-drivers, the schedule is once a week; for camel-drivers, once in thirty days; for sailors, once in six months; for disciples of the wise, once a week, because the study of Torah weakens their strength. It is the practice of disciples of the wise to have conjugal relations each Friday night." (The Code of Maimonides, Book 4 on Women, Chapter 14, Section 1.) Maimonides, probably influenced by Aristotle, states that the disciples of the wise, i.e., scholars and intellectuals, have a weaker sex drive. That is his personal opinion and there are many who would disagree.

"To give his wife pleasure." Sex manuals have become increasingly popular in America. In reaction against Anglo-Saxon prudity they

presence, and *it is an instrument for peace in the world,* as it stands written, 'and thou shalt know that thy tent is in peace: and thou shalt visit thy habitation and not sin.' (Job 5:24). It

frequently seem only to be concerned with "performance technique." Most of them are aware of the psychological and emotional aspects of sexual relationships, but none seem to be aware of the religious dimensions of sex. That sex is a Mitsvah is beyond them. These authors who will tell you everything you always wanted to know but were ashamed to ask, should read Iggeret Hakodesh (A Letter on Holiness), a sex manual by a thirteenth century Kabbalist (Rabbi Moses ben Nakhman, or according to Professor Gershon Scholem, Rabbi Joseph ibn Gikatilia).

The sixth chapter of Iggeret Hakodesh entitled "On the Quality of the Act" states "Therefore engage her first in conversation that puts her heart and mind at ease and gladdens her. Thus your mind and your intent will be in harmony with hers. Speak words which arouse her to passion, union, love, desire and eroticism and words which elicit attitudes of reverence for God, piety and modesty. Tell her of pious and good women who gave birth to fine and pure children... Speak with her words, some of love, some of erotic passion, some of piety and reverence... Never may you force her, for in such union the Divine Presence cannot abide. Your intent is then different from hers, and her mood is not in accord with yours. Quarrel not with her, nor strike her, in connection with this act; as our Sages taught. "Just as a lion tramples and devours and has no shame, so a boorish man strikes and copulates and has no shame." Rather win her over with words of graciousness and seductiveness... Hurry not to arouse passion until her mood is ready; begin in love; let her vaginal secreting take place first..." All this is done to fulfill the Mitsvah so he can give his wife pleasure. because it is due to her that God's presence rests on him.

"It is an instrument for peace in the world." Most people believe that the sexual relationship between husband and wife is purely personal. It is a private expression of their subjective feelings. But the Zohar teaches that it is much more than that. It is a Mitsvah. But how can the Mitsvah of sex be an instrument for world peace? To understand the answer it is necessary first to understand the mystical nature of Mitsvot (the plural of Mitsvah). Religion is, of course, subjective. What you believe affects how you behave and who you become. But religion is more than just your personal subjective feelings and beliefs.

There is a God. We not only seek him; He seeks us. Almost everyone believes in God. But what do they believe? They see God as an insurance policy or as a cosmic bellboy. He should be there when they need him. Yet where are they each and every day when God needs them to help sanctify the world? For the majority, God is a giver, not a demander. "Do not ask what you can do for God; ask only what he can do for you" should be their motto. The Jewish tradition has always stressed man's obligations to his fellow man and to God. We are all partners with God in the Divine journey. We have an important role to play in the future development of the Messianic Age. (See Chapter XI. "The Coming of the Messianic Age").

Every rational person can see how the Mitsvot that apply to relations between one person and another help improve our society. Jews have been disproportionately involved in almost every movement to improve the economic, political, and cultural situation of society. Jews made up 30 to 50 percent of the volunteers for the Peace Corps during the 1960's. They were 40 to 50 percent of the civil rights activists who journeyed into the South during the late '50's and early '60's. Although most Jews have above average incomes and educations, they consistently support government-welfare programs for the poor and uneducated.

All sociological studies show that Jews also support the freedoms described in the Bill of Rights to a greater degree than any other group of Americans. Jews contribute proportionately more money to charities, both Jewish and general, than non-Jews. Very few Jews are serving time in jail, and when Jews do break the law, it rarely involves crimes of violence. All this means that Jews are among the best citizens in the country. It is clear, therefore, that the Jewish tradition has led them, whether consciously or not, to the performance of many Mitsvot between one person and another. The net effect of all these Mitsvot has been the improvement of society, and they therefore are instruments for promoting justice and peace in the world.

But how can such a private Mitsvah as that of sexual relationship between husband and wife be an instrument for peace in the world? The fulfillment of this Mitsvah involves a relationship between man and God. In order to understand the cosmic significance of all the Mitsvot we must examine more closely the Mitsvot themselves.

The Torah, according to Rabbinic tradition, contains 613 Mitsvot. No one could possibly do them all. Some apply only to farmers (Leviticus 19:9, 10 or Deuteronomy 24:19-21), or to a King of Israel (Deuteronomy 17:14-18). Some apply only to a woman (Deuteronomy 21:10-14) or to a man (Deuteronomy 20:10). And some apply only to a time of war (Deuteronomy 20:19-20). The inability to perform the latter Mitsvah due to the elimination of warfare, would be in itself a Mitsvah. In any case, the essential thing is our willingness to accept our obligation to carry out as many of God's commandments as possible.

Everyone has heard of the Ten Commandments. Most people think that is all there are. They ignore, or are ignorant of, the other 603 commandments. Perhaps they think, or were taught, that the others are less important. How can anyone say that a commandment like "Thou shalt love thy neighbor as thyself"(Leviticus 19:18), or "Thou shalt not deliver unto a master, a slave who has escaped from his master" (Deuteronomy 23:16), or "Thou shalt surely open thy hand to thy poor and needy brother" (Deuteronomy 15:11), are less important than the Ten Commandments. In fact, the Torah never says that this commandment is really important and this one is not.

The commandment to protect a runaway slave, and the South's challenge to it in the Fugitive Slave Act, were among the immediate conflicts leading up to the American Civil War. If Southern Protestants had followed this Mitsvah as well as the other Mitsvot in the Torah that relate to slavery, the Civil War would have been avoided, as would the present racial crisis. These Mitsvot surely would have been instruments for peace in our society.

There are people who say that while the ethical commandments of the Bible are important and must be observed, the ritual commandments are less important and don't have to be observed. But all of the Mitsvot are ethical, even if we don't understand their full meaning, because they are expressive of the Divine Will. The Torah teaches "Thou shalt not muzzle the ox when he treads out the corn" (Deuteronomy 25:4). It is true that it is more efficient and profitable to do this and therefore it would be better for mankind. But we have responsibilities to nature also, and to avoid unnecessary animal suffering is a Mitsvah. Who can say if torturing an animal by making it work so close to the food that it hungers for, and preventing it from eating, is a greater or a lesser sin than lying or stealing. The Torah doesn't make such a judgment.

Most people who make the distinction between the more important and the less important commandments, do so because they want to avoid observing some of the commandments, which they then designate as lesser. This is what Jesus Josephson meant when he said "Whosoever shall break one of these least commandments, and shall teach men so, he shall be called the least in the kingdom of heaven; but whoever shall do and teach them, the same shall be called great in the kingdom of heaven" (Matthew 5:19).

may be questioned, *is it a sin if he fails to go in to his wife?* It is a sin, for in his failure, he detracts from the honor of the heavenly mate who was given him by reason of his wife. *Secondly, if his wife should conceive,* the heavenly partner

"Is it a sin if he fails to go in to his wife?" Yes, it is a sin. Celibacy and abstinence are not Mitsvot. Neither would they be considered "natural." Birth control by abstention is much less natural than is birth control with a pill or a prophylactic. Modern sociological studies have shown that American Jews practice birth control to a greater extent, and with greater success, than any other group in the United States. Recent surveys have estimated that as many as one-quarter of all children who were born were not planned or desired. The number of unplanned Jewish children is only five to ten percent.

The creation of a child demands more responsibility than any other human act. It is for this reason that sexual relations outside of marriage were so strongly condemned in the past. Even today, with birth control methods so readily available thirty to forty percent of couples involved in premarital intercourse are not practicing birth control. Especially among teenagers who lack the maturity and responsibility to handle their sexual potentiality, sex without birth control is the norm. A survey of 4,600 teenage girls for the U. S. government's Commision on Population Growth and The American Future, found that 17 percent of white 16 year old girls had sexual relations, and only 41 percent of them had used birth control. By age 18, one third of white girls had sexual experience, and only 54 percent of them were using birth control. Even at age 19 when most girls would consider themselves adult, 35 percent of the girls having sexual relations were not using contraception.

No couple that lacks the responsibility to practice birth control is mature enough to engage in sexual relations. Usually their excuse is that they hadn't planned to have sexual relations and somehow it had just happened. The truth is, most of these couples are too embarrassed, ambivalent, or guilt-ridden, to admit to themselves or to each other that they are going to have sexual relations. So they cop out and claim it "just happened."

"Secondly, if his wife should conceive." Conception is not regarded as the primary reason for cohabitation according to the Zohar. Is the possibility of conception essential to make intercourse a Mitsvah? No, it is not.

bestows upon the child a holy soul: for this covenant is called the convenant of the Holy One.

"Hence, *a man should be as zealous to enjoy this joy as to enjoy the joy of the Shabat,* at which time is consummated the union of the sages with their wives. Thus, 'Thou shalt know that

It is a Mitsvah to have sex even when the wife cannot conceive, as for example when she is already pregnant. To this very day, there are doctors who advise, and people who believe, that intercourse during pregnancy is harmful to the fetus and should be avoided. This is not true. The claim is a rationalization for avoiding intercourse used by people who do not regard sex as a Mitsvah. In ancient times, it was thought that a pregnant woman could still conceive and that the resultant growth of a second fetus would injure the first, or cause a premature birth. This is probably the theory used by thinkers like Aristotle and Pliny to account for premature and/or deformed births.

The Talmud, however, states, "a woman cannot conceive while already pregnant." Nevertheless, there is an opinion in the Talmud which probably was influenced by Greek or Persian medical science to the effect that during the first three months of pregnancy, marital intercourse is dangerous to the woman and to the fetus. During the middle three months, it is injurious to the mother, but benficial to the fetus. However, the Talmud notes, "during the last three months, it is beneficial for both the woman and the fetus, since on account of it the child becomes well formed and of strong vitality." During the last three months a woman's figure changes drastically, and she is anxious about how "ugly" she appears. This is the time when a wife most needs her husband's attention. The Sefer Mitsvot Katan in discussing Mitsvah # 285 states, "when his wife is pregnant, it is a Mitsvah to cause her thus to be happy if she feels she is desirous."

"Zealous to Enjoy this Joy." The Jewish teaching that sex is both holy and joyful is in direct opposition to the Christian doctrine of original sin, which is really nothing but the Apostle Paul's antisexual attitudes raised to a cosmic level. The doctrine was largely formulated by Augustine (355–430 C.E.), a bishop in North Africa, whose writings suggest he suffered from severe sexual hangups.

Augustine taught that before Adam ate of the Tree of Knowledge in the Garden of Eden, his sexual drive was completely under control. It never compelled him to acts against his better interests or moral values. His sexual drive always followed his conscious will.

Then, according to Augustine's view, pride and egotism led Adam and Eve to sin. They ate of the Tree of Knowledge and "they knew they were naked." They became conscious of a new, destructive impulse which had been generated by their rebellious act against the will of God. This impulse was lust.

From that moment according to Augustine, their sexual drive no longer was subordinate to their rational will. This consequence of their sin of disobedience is transmitted from generation to generation because every human being is born as a result of lust.

In the sixth century a monk, Pope Gregory I, added to the already serious conflicts Christians were suffering regarding sex. He taught that it was not the act of sex which was sinful, but the sensual pleasure accompanying the act. Procreation was natural, he felt, but God did not want you to enjoy it. Judaism rejects these ideas in total.

A Man Should be as Zealous to Enjoy this Joy as to Enjoy the Joy of the Shabbat." By the Middle Ages, official Christian antagonism to sex had reached such heights that most priests advocated sexual abstinence during the Christian holidays so they would not be profaned. Some priests went so far as to recommend abstinence on Thursdays in memory of the arrest of Jesus; on Fridays in memory of his death; on Saturdays in honor of the Virgin; on Sundays in honor of the Resurrection; and on Mondays in memory of departed souls. For their followers, sex could be kosher only on Tuesdays and Wednesdays.

Throughout Europe during the Middle Ages, the Church elevated celibacy and the monastic state to the highest prestige. During this time and into the period of the Renaissance, when troubadors sang their ballads of romantic love, the ideal embodied in their songs was "to love pure and chaste from afar."

The Jewish minority in Christian Europe strongly dissented from the Christian sex ethic. In the same century (the 13th) that the Zohar with its teachings of Divine Sex was edited and a wonderful sex manual, the Iggeret Hakodesh was written by a famous Kabbalist Rabbi Moses Ben Nakhman, Pope Innocent III declared that "the sexual act was itself so shameful as to be inherently wicked."

The Iggeret Hakodesh specifically rejects Christian sex morality and states that "sexual intercourse is holy and pure when carried on properly, at the proper time, and with the proper intentions. No one should claim that it is ugly or unseemly. God forbid! For intercourse is called 'knowing' (Genesis 4:1) and not in vain is it called thus... Understand that if marital intercourse did not partake of great holiness, it would not be called thy tent is in peace,' for the presence accompanies you and sojourns in your house, and for this reason 'Thou shalt visit thy habitation and not sin,' in *Gladly carrying out the religious duty to have conjugal intercourse before the presence."*

'knowing.' The matter is not as our Rabbi and Guide Moses Maimonides supposed, in his book *Guide for the Perplexed,* where he endorses Aristotle's teaching that the sense of touch is unworthy. God forbid. That Greek nogoodnik is wrong and his error proceeds from his view of the universe.

Had he believed that one God created the world he would not have slipped into such an error. But we who have the Torah, and believe that God created all in His wisdom, do not believe that he created anything inherently ugly or unseemly. If we were to say that intercourse is repulsive then we blaspheme God who made the genitals... Hands can write a Sefer Torah and are then honorable and exalted; hands, too, can perform evil deeds and then they are ugly. So the genitals... Whatever ugliness there is comes from how a man uses them. All organs of the body are neutral; the use made of them determines whether they are holy or unholy... Therefore marital intercourse, under proper circumstances, is an exalted matter... Now you can understand what our Rabbis meant when they declared that when a husband unites with his wife in holiness, the Shekenah abides with them."

Thus, the Zohar compares the joy of fulfilling the Mitsvah of intercourse to the joy of fulfilling the Mitsvah of Shabbat. When husband and wife make love on a Jewish holiday they fulfill a double Mitsvah. This is why the Sages always combined sex, prayer, and study on Shabbat.

"Gladly carrying out the religious duty to have conjugal intercourse before the presence." In all the teachings of the Rabbis we find the stress on proper attitude and circumstances. Sexual intercourse is only holy when it is between husband and wife. Modern society has gone much too far in its revolt against the degrading of sex in the Christian tradition. Americans elevate and exalt sex as the be all, and end all of life. Sex is publicly displayed on stage and screen. In our consumer oriented society sex is treated as a product to be marketed. It is also used by advertisers as a tool. Modesty is ridiculed. If you have something valuable it must be displayed in the market place according to American philosophy.

Social pressure to obtain sexual experience is so widespread and demanding that an eighteen or nineteen year old virgin, either male or female, feels defensive, and may even be ashamed about his, or her inexperience. Other young people engage in sexual activities not because they are in love and married, but because they think that if they don't, they won't be considered normal, or with it.

From the extreme of Paul and Augustine we have gone to the other extreme of the Playboy philosophy. Here sex is regarded as a game. The most important thing is to score. And the more victories you chalk up the better a player you are. *Variety rather than stability is the goal.* Technique is what counts. Each partner must perform according to the exaggerated standards that are constantly presented in novels and films. The fear of failure poisons many people's personalities. Rather than being a way of "knowing" another person, the Playboy sex ethic is only a way of having fun and fulfilling yourself.

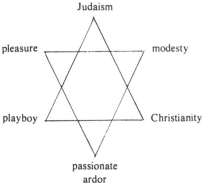

The relationship between the three different philosophies of sexual morality can be diagrammed in a triangle. At the right is the traditional Christian repression of sex. Opposite it, to the left, is the American playboy's exultation in sex. Above both of them is the Jewish sanctification of sex.

If we intersect this triangle with another one we form a star of David. This shows us the relationships between the three attitudes to sex. Christianity and Judaism share a pro-modesty value which is directly opposite the playboy philosophy. Judaism and the playboy philosophy share a pro-pleasure attitude towards sex which is the direct opposite of the Christian position. Christianity and the playboy philosophy share the belief that the essence of sex is its passionate ardor, although one interprets it positively and the other negatively. The emphasis on passion and ardor is opposite the Jewish view of sex as a responsible Mitsvah.

The mystical symbolism of the sexual organs is revealed in a passage from a book in the Zohar called Idra Rabbah (The Great Holy Assembly p. 142a.).

"It is taught in the Book of Concealment that the male was extended and established in his various formations. The genital of the female was established, a pure covering, and also the pure genital member of the male. *The member extends through 248 ,worlds:* all of them depend on the orifice of the member that is

"The member extends through 248 worlds." The male genital is the penis. The 248 worlds refers to the 248 positive Mitsvot. As we know, the Holy Torah contains 613 commandments; 365 are negative, and 248 are positive. Most people observe many of the negative commandments without even being conscious that they are observing a Mitsvah. Thus, the Mitsvah not to eat any animal that has died a natural death (Deuteronomy 14:21) is observed by almost everyone in the United States because Federal and State Pure Food and Drug Acts prohibit such animals from being cut up and sold.

It is, of course, always better to observe a Mitsvah, than not to observe it. However, the best observance is coupled with the conscious awareness of performing the Mitsvah for "the sake of heaven." A Jew who doesn't eat pork because he doesn't like the taste of ham or bacon observes this Mitsvah (Deuteronomy 14:8), but much superior are the people who would love to eat pork products but refrain from doing so because they desire even more to fulfill the Divine Will. Vegetarians fulfill all of the Mitsvot relating to kosher food. If they also study the Mitsvot of Kashrut and the laws of mercy for all living creatures, they add a great deal of merit and sanctity to their vegetarianism. Yet even without conscious awareness it is still meritorious and beneficial to observe the Mitsvot.

The 248 positive Mitsvot, on the other hand, require much greater conscious awareness. Each one involves doing something (the Torah contains no Mitsvot of belief because no person, no state, no church, no book, not even God Himself can command you to believe something you do not believe). In the Jewish tradition, it is deed, and not creed, that is important. It is better to perform a Mitsvah for the wrong reason than not to perform the Mitsvah at all.

For example, it is better for a wealthy person to make a contribution to a hospital or a university although his primary motive might be seeing his name written on the building or trying to impress other people. Neither the called *Y*. When this *Y is uncovered, in the circumcision,* the supernal kindness is revealed. The genital member itself is kindness, called after and depending upon its orifice. It is not

student who learns nor the patient who is healed, derives any less benefit from the facilities according to the motive of the donor. If, however, the charitable contributions had been sought under the more pure ideal of an anonymous donation and that had resulted, as of course it would, in smaller donations, and therefore less adequate facilities, the patient or the student would be harmed.

It is for this reason, that motive while extremely important in elevating a Mitsvah, is not essential for determining that any act is or is not a Mitsvah. On the other hand, according to the Rabbis, motive always counts on a person's behalf if his motive was good but the outcome of his acts was not. But I have digressed.

The meaning of the penis which extends through 248 worlds of positive Mitsvot is that each positive Mitsvah influences a world in another solar system somewhere in our galaxy. The more often each one of us performs a Mitsvah, and the more people who perform the Mitsvah here on our planet, the greater is the improvement תיקון (Tikun) that occurs on other planets, on other worlds. Of course, the creatures who live on the other worlds also have their own Torah (which is composed of the same letters as our own, but is arranged differently to make different words, sentences, and Mitsvot) and when they observe their Mitsvot, it helps improve our world.

"Y is Uncovered in the Circumcision." The Hebrew letter Yod is the smallest letter in the Hebrew alphabet, just as the penis is the smallest of the extremities of the male body. The Yod also has the shape of a penis. It looks like this: י (Knowledge of the Hebrew alphabet is essential to any person who wishes to understand the Kabbalah. Most Jewish children attend Hebrew school for three or four years in addition to their religious school classes. A non-Jew should not despair, however, for most synagogues offer beginning Hebrew classes for adults in the evenings. These are usually open to non-members, including non-Jews, so just call around and find out where and when they are being held). The letter Yod is the tenth letter in the Hebrew alphabet, and so it stands for the number ten; the ten emanations that gave rise to our universe. In the circumcision, the natural body is altered to express our willingness to fulfill God's Mitsvot with all out heart, with all our soul, and with all our might.

It is true that today many Gentiles are also circumcised (almost all males in the United States, but very few in Europe or South America) because they believe that it is medically beneficial in reducing the chances of suffering from cancer of the penis. Circumcision also reduces the occurrence of cancer of the cervix for the wives of circumcised men. This is medically correct and undoubtedly beneficial. It is however absurd to maintain that either Abraham or Moses knew about cancer three or four thousand years ago, and so decreed the rite of circumcision. Some people try to explain the laws of Kashrut as ways in which wise leaders, who had observed the harmful effects of trichinosis, etc. tried to protect their followers. This is absurd. Circumcision on the eighth day is the fulfillment of a Mitsvah and a sign of the covenant between God and the Jewish people, as it says in Genesis 17:1-14.

Of course, it is not surprising that circumcision is good for our health. All of God's Mitsvot are good for people, both spiritually and physically. In fact, we are just beginning to learn of the benefits that people derive from observing the Mitsvot. As scientists learn more and more, they will undoubtedly discover many additional benefits of circumcision, kosher food, etc. However, to keep a Mitsvah for selfish reasons of personal benefit is not nearly as worthy as to observe it because it is the way of fulfilling the Divine dimension of man's life. Nevertheless, it is better to keep the Mitsvot for selfish reasons than not to keep them at all. More and more young people realize the need for a spiritual diet. Let them read the words of Rabbi Rubin:

"Food is not only the basis of physical health but also of mental health. It has been said with truth that 'Man is what he eats.'

"Just as contaminated food may communicate physical disease which was carried by the animal, so does unclean meat transfer to the body the animal instincts which reside in the flesh and blood of the animal.

"We Jews have been destined to carry the torch of God's light upon this earth which He has revealed in the Torah. For this Divine purpose we have been equipped with special safeguards to preserve the nobility of our character and preserve the purity of our Divine soul. Among these safeguards, the dietary laws are fundamental.

"If our body is to be the instrument of our soul, as it is destined to be, it must be fed on those foods which the Creator has prescribed for it, and must abstain from all foods that contaminate it.

"In the world of vegetation, everything has been made permissible for our consumption, for vegetables contain no adverse substances.

"In the animal world, however, there are animals which have savage instincts, cruel or otherwise bad habits. Such are all carnivorous (meat eating) animals and birds of prey. Their flesh has been forbidden to us, so *called kindness* until this orifice has been uncovered. As soon as this occurred, he was called perfect, as it is written (Gen. 17:1), 'Walk before me and be perfect.' It is also written (II Sam. 22:24), 'I will be perfect with him, and I will guard myself from sin.' What is the subject matter in the two halves of this verse? It tells us that *He who uncovers this Y and takes care not to allow it to enter into a foreign domain* will be perfect in the world-to-come and will be bound up in the bond of life. *What is a 'Foreign Domain'?* As it is written (Mal. 2:11), *'He married the*

that we should not acquire those savage animal instincts inherent in their flesh and blood. Only certain species of animals, which have both Kashruth characetristics, i.e., a) chewing the cud, and b) having cloven hoofs, (domestic cattle, sheep, goats) and certain species of domestic fowl, are permitted as food for us. These are herbivorous (vegetarians) and are closest to the vegetable world; they are tame, non-aggressive, and possess no cruel habits. Their flesh is kosher (after preparation in compliance with the laws of Kashruth)."

"Called Kindness." The male organ is referred to in the Zohar and in other Kabbalistic literature as חסד Hesed, "Kindness". Note the tremendous difference in attitude inherent in this name compared to the attitudes inherent in the usual way the sexual organs are referred to in the western world. In the culture of the western world, the slang words for the sexual organs are frequently derogatory or slighting. When people curse or swear, they call each other names that refer to the various sexual organs or to the act of intercourse itself.

This reveals the perverted view of sex in the culture of the western world where it is generally considered something dirty, something debased, and that to describe people in sexual imagery is to degrade and insult them. If people had the elevated and exalted concept of sex that is called for in the Zohar, they would realize that a description or an image involving sexual imagery is always a positive, beautiful image. It would be used to praise and not to denigrate.

"He who uncovers this Y and takes care not to allow it to enter into a foreign domain will be perfect." The Y (Yod), as we have seen, refers to the penis and the uncovering of the Yod to the rite of circumcision. What does it mean that we should take care that it should not enter a foreign domain? As the Zohar states in the next sentence. *"What is a foreign domain? He married the daughter of a strange*

daughter of a Strange God." Therefore is it written 'I will be perfect with him' — Because he is perfect through the revelation

god." This means that a Jew is not permitted to marry or have sexual relations with the children of a non-Jew. As it says in the Torah, (Deuteronomy 7:3 and 4), "You shall not make marriages with them: Your daughter you shall not give to his son, nor should you take his daughter for your son. For they will turn away your children from following me, and they will serve other gods."

The opposition in the Jewish community to marriage with non-Jews (where the non-Jews do not become part of the Jewish people and where the children are not raised in the Jewish community), goes back to the days of Abraham (Genesis 24:3). The Jewish people have always been a very small minority in the world and if they had intermarried with the non-Jews surrounding them, they would have disappeared thousands of years ago.

If they had intermarried during Biblical days and disappeared, Christianity would never have been born. If they had intermarried during the days of the Roman Empire and disappeared, Islam would never have been born. If they intermarry and disappear now, the Messianic Age will never come about. The existence of the Jewish people is necessary for the fulfillment of the goal of human history which is the creation of the Kingdom of God here on earth. The Zohar says that a person who observes Jewish solidarity by marrying a Jew (or a Gentile who becomes Jewish) will be perfect in the world to come.

Why does it not say he shall be perfect in this world also? Because the majority of Jews do marry other Jews and we cannot say that all the Jews who fulfill this very important Mitzvah also fulfill the other six hundred and twelve mitzvot. The Zohar is telling us that a Jew may fail to fulfill many Mitzvot in this world, and therefore be denied the spiritual fulfillment achievable in this world, however in the world to come, the Mitzvah of "be fruitful and multiply and continue the Jewish people" having been fulfilled in this world, guarantees a form of perfection in his or her existence in the world to come.

I must also mention that one of my teachers, Rabbi Jacob—may his memory be a blessing—taught me. The Messiah, the Son of David, will be the descendant not just of King David (i.e., biologically a descendant of the Jewish leader) but on his mother's side, he would be a descendant of a convert to Judaism, just as the original David was descended from Ruth, a convert to Judaism. Therefore, as we approach the final stages of the Messianic Age, conversion to Judaism will increase substantially. In the of the Y. Then will he guard himself from sin.

At the time that the genital member developed in the male, the aspect of rigor developed in the female, *from those rigorous powers of her left side.* It sank deeply into the female in a certain place and is denoted by her *'Nakedness',* the covering of her entire body. The place considered the greatest 'Nakedness' of all is that set aside for the concealment of kindness, the genital

generation or two following one of those conversions, will be born the man who eventually will be selected by the Holy One to play the dominant role in the fulfillment of the Messianic Age.

"From those rigorous powers of her left side." Of course in metaphysics the male refers to the Sefirah that gives, and the female refers to the Sefirah that receives. Since mankind is a microcosm, human acts have cosmic significance. The inner organs in the female which are the Side (Dimension) of Judgment are established when Mercy expanded in the male and penetrated the female. This teaches us that the rigorous characteristics of justice, discipline, reason, and duty are founded on the soft emotions of love, mercy, kindness, and empathy. They are not opposite but different dimensions of the same reality. Too many people think they are tolerent and forgiving, when in reality they are indifferent and unconcerned. They confuse mercy with indulgence, and broadmindedness with lack of commitment.

The paragraph that precedes the one we are studying, teaches that "the side of the male is formed with 248 formations within, some internal and some external. Some are mercy, while others are judgment. All those of judgment are united with the judgment of the back part, from where the female is extended." The 248 formations refer to the 248 positive mitzvot; some are internal (i.e., personal), some are external (i.e., social), some are merciful (soft), while others are judgmental (demanding self-discipline and cold logic). All the 248 apply to the male, but those positive mitsvot that have a fixed time for performance apply to the female only if she desires. The 365 negative mitzvot (the dimension of judgment) apply to the male and female. Thus all the duties from the female apply to the male but not all the duties from the male apply to the female. She is less in need of positive Mitzvot because she is superior to the male.

"Nakedness." The Zohar describes five types of nakedness based on a statement in the Talmud, (Berachot 24a). These five are in the dimension of judgment and extend to the two hundred and forty-eight subordinated

member of the male. In this way is her rigor mitigated and assuaged. Since it contains the five powers of rigor, this is accomplished by the kindness that comprehends the five degrees of kindness. *Kindness is Right, Rigor is Left.* The one is mitigated by the other, and he can be called adam, complete on the two sides.

paths, which as we have already discussed are the positive mitzvot. The five most alluring or stimulating aspects of women, according to the Talmud, are; "her voice, her hair, her legs, her hands, and her feet. The hand of a woman and the foot of a woman have not been openly discussed among the sages, but they actually provide a greater opportunity for sin, greater even than the other three." Her hands signify power and discipline. Her feet are the object of adoration and humility. (Isaiah 49:22-3).

"Kindness is the Right, Rigor is the Left." The division between right and left is one that is found in many religious and mystical systems. It represents an insight into the dual nature of reality, the objective versus the subjective, the rational versus the emotional.

Modern science is just beginning to learn that this dualism is rooted in the physical structure of the brain. The brain's division into two hemispheres is visible to the naked eye. The functions of the two halves of the brain, the right and the left hemisphere, are not mere duplicates or even parallels to one another, although it is true that some parts of the brain do seem to act as back-up units for other parts.

Recent scientific research has found that the left hemisphere is usually associated with verbal and sequential processes (cause and effect, logic,etc.,) while the right hemisphere is usually associated with spatial, musical, and emotional processes. Several recent studies have also shown that meditation is associated with increased right-hemisphere activity. Without becoming sidetracked by a discussion of the nervous system, it is interesting to note that religious mystics gained insights into the duality between the right and left sides of reality, millenia prior to the recent scientific observations of human physiology.

THE SECRETS OF CREATION

In a very real sense the creation of the universe was the beginning of each of us. Our "roots" and the very atoms of our bodies go back to that beginning of beginnings.

But for all the mystical revelations, philosophic reasoning, and scientific study devoted to that subject, little consensus has been reached. Religious scholars, philosophers, and scientists continue to battle over their pet theories.

A persistent hotspot in the controversies is the Biblical description of creation: Is it literally true, symbolically true, or only a meaningless folk tale? Amusingly, many of the loudest of the combatants only *think* they know what the Bible actually says on the subject.

Was the world created in seven days? Did Adam and Eve live in the Garden of Eden until they ate an apple and fell from the Grace of God? Fundamentalists say yes to these questions in the mistaken belief that this represents the Bible's history of creation.

In fact, the Bible contains two completely different descriptions of creation. Each incorporates a different perspective, an entirely different approach, to the nature of reality. One of them, the Garden of Eden version, is an allegory addressing itself to the development of pre humans into humans, and the value of family life, stressing the dignity of women and woman's partnership with man in the history of civilization, and her role in bringing humanity closer to the image of God.

The Bible's first description of Creation (Genesis I-II:3) states that vegetation—grass and herbs and fruitbearing trees—was created on the third day, fish and fowl on the fifth day; and on the sixth day cattle and animals of all kinds were created. Then after everything else, human beings were brought forth, male and female simultaneously. Finally, on the seventh day, God rested and ordained the Sabbath.

The second account begins with the creation of man. This description (Genesis II:4 to the end of Genesis III)says there were *no* shrubs in the field when God created man. *Then* He planted a Garden, and *then* He caused the trees to grow, and *then* He caused the animals to be created. Finally, at the very end, according to this perspective, God created woman. Hidden in the difference between these two accounts is a profound mystery.

The two different descriptions became entangled, the first version ending in the same chapter which contains the begining of the second, because thousands of years after the Torah was first written down the Bible was divided into chapters, and the verses were numbered, (during the Middle Ages) by men who did not realize they were dealing with two separate accounts. The original Torah Scroll does not contain page numbers, verse numbers, chapter numbers, or even punctuation marks. This is one of the reasons the Torah has been translated in so many different ways. You can see what the original Torah looked like by visiting any synagogue on a Saturday morning when the Torah, handwritten on parchment as it has been for over three thousand years, will be read.

Not only were these two accounts written by different people, the attitudes and interests of the two authors differed greatly. Genesis I-II:3 is the description of creation from the objective, universal perspective of the scientific mind. And it relates well to the theories of creation that have been developed by contemporary astronomers. About fifteen to twenty billion years ago, the most widely held theory goes, the entire matter of the universe was compressed under infinite pressure, at a single point, without any dimensions.

The mass was composed entirely of subatomic particles compressed together so tightly that its gravitational force prevented light from radiating outward. The universe was one immeasurable "black hole." Then came the "Big Bang," an explosion beyond description, even in an age that has witnessed the force of a hydrogen bomb. The explosion propelled subatomic particles outward, reducing the gravitational force sufficiently to permit the radiation of light. Expansion was so rapid that in the first moments of creation, the temperature at the perimeter of the universe dropped from billions to only millions of degrees.

The process of expansion has been going on ever since, and still continues today, so that the time it now takes light to travel from one end of the universe to the other, at a speed of one hundred and eighty-six thousand miles a second, is more than ten billion years. During the initial expansion, through random collisions, the subatomic particles formed atoms of hydrogen (the most simple of the atoms), creating clouds of hydrogen gas that eventually began to condense, through gravitational attraction, into the billions of stars in our galaxy, and into the other billions of galaxies in the universe.

The Torah tells us that on the second day the מים *mayim* was separated into the upper and lower *mayim*. The Hebrew word *mayim* (which in ordinary usage means water) is closely related to the word שמים *shamayim* which is translated as heavens or universe. But in this context *mayim* refers to the clouds of hydrogen gas which, when they condensed on the fourth day, became the billions of galaxies, which with their millions of solar systems, comprise the universe.

Size determined whether a gas cloud became a star or merely a planet. At any size, a gas cloud heats up as it contracts; the larger the cloud the higher its resultant internal temperature. At a certain mass the internal temperature reaches twenty million degrees, igniting the atomic reaction that creates a star. Below that mass, no atomic reaction takes place, and condensation eventually cooled the mass; forming planetary crusts. One theory holds that planets condensed before the stars due to their smaller size. This theory parallels the first description of creation in the Torah which says that dry land-that is the earth and the other planets-appeared on the third day and that on the fourth day the stars and the sun were created.

Our sun was not formed until ten to fifteen billion years after the Beginning, the "Big Bang." By that time, millions of stars with their solar systems had not only been created but had already burned out. Most amazing of all, the heavier atoms of our bodes were at one time (five to ten billion years ago) actually a part of those exploding stars.

However, it should be pointed out that the first description of creation seems to be in error, from the point of view of contemporary scientific knowledge, in stating that trees and grass appeared on earth prior to the creation of the sun, the moon, and the stars. This apparent error serves to remind us that the Torah is not just a scientific text, and should not be used as a text for detailed scientific information.

The first description, of creation, demonstrates the perspective of science; it begins with creation, lists the major sequence of evolutionary events, ends with the creation of mankind, the highest form of animal life on earth, and is followed by the creation of the Sabbath, the highest form of spiritual life on earth.

The second account is written from the personal, emotional perspective. It begins with the creation of man. All of its references are to mankind's experiences. Note the wording: "...no shrub of the field was yet on earth, and there was no *man* to till the ground." The emphasis is on mankind. From the scientific point of view, the earth and planet life existed for over a billion years without men to till the ground and to manipulate the environment and to subdue the world. Mankind is a very late comer. But, psychologists tell us, from the subjective view point of the individual, creation begins with your own awareness. The world begins for you, with your birth, and ends with your death. Emotionally, it is difficult to become involved with what happened a hundred million years ago. What matters the most to you is what touches your life, your experiences.

We can look at the world from the perspective of science and say that there are three or four billion people in the world, and in terms of survival of the species it does not matter if a few persons live or die. But from the subjective perspective, if someone you love is among those who die, that death is important.

This is the perspective of Genesis II, the subjective, personal, point of view. Note that in this account, humanity is created monosexually. In the beginning, God created man alone. Subsequently, God created animals and the birds for the purpose of providing man with companionship. However, man still was lonely, so God made woman from a bone taken from the body of the man. And because woman was made of his body, man yearns to be joined with her and to cleave unto her. Again, note the psychological perspective of this version. In Genesis I, the male-female difference, like the development of sex in nature, simply is the biological means of reproduction. In Genesis II, however, the female is the necessary complement and completion of the male; it is only when they are joined together through love and sex that they become whole. Genesis II provides us with an allegorical explanation of the reason a boy and a girl, when they mature, must leave the families they love, and find mates, completing themselves sexually and emotionally.

The story of the Garden of Eden is one the most misunderstood and misinterpreted allegories in the history of mankind. The story starts with the last verse in Chapter II and continues to the end of Chapter III. Most people believe it is the story of a man and a woman who lived in a sort of Hawaiian paradise until the woman ate an apple and got the man to eat it. This caused the landlord to get mad and kick the two of them out, punishing them and all their descendants too, so that, due to their actions, we still suffer the penalty of death.

This interpretation is completely wrong. First of all, at the end of the allegory (III:22), God says, "Man has become as one of us to know good and evil." The Torah is saying that mankind became like God by eating from the Tree of the Knowledge of Good and Evil and so, like God, came to know Good and Evil. The fact is that at the end of the allegory, mankind has become more like God than it had been at the allegory's beginning.

This indicates that the allegory is not about the fall of mankind but about the rise of mankind's awareness.

We must analyze this allegory carefully to understand what it really means. The Torah says that man and woman were naked and they were not ashamed. This statement teaches us that they were living in a state of nature as animals still do. Living in a state of nature, animals mate in the open. They do not object if other animals watch while they mate. Many mate indiscriminately.When the female is in heat, she will accept all males of her species who approach her.

Humans are different. Although specific customs vary from culture to culture, in every human community, there are, and there always have been, customs indicating a feeling of shame and propriety regarding sexual behavior. Sexual relations between men and women are regarded as being private. Clothing covering the parts of the body related to sex is a symbol of this sense of privacy. Among the other primates, there is no similar sense of a need for privacy,or for moral and sexual propriety.Thus clothing and propriety in terms of sexual conduct can be considered an unique characteristic of human communities.

However, the state of man and woman in the Garden of Eden was that of animals or infants, who feel no need for sexual privacy and therefore are not ashamed of their nakedness. We will understand the meaning of this allegory better if we compare mankind in the Garden to an infant, and what happened to Adam and Eve to the process of growing up, acquiring moral knowledge, and independent judgment.

This allegory, of course, was not really concerned with a guy named Adam and his girlfriend, Eve. Remember that Adam and Eve gave birth to three sons, one of whom was killed. The other two married, but whom did they marry? Fundamentalists, maintaining that Adam and Eve were the only people God had created, were forced to say their sons married sisters, pointing out that ordinarily the birth of females was not recorded in the Torah. The marriage of brothers and sisters is incest. And incest was prohibited not only by the Jews but by the general population of every society that has ever been upon the earth.

Creation was not simply a matter of one man and one woman who had the names of Adam and Eve. God created mankind.That is to say, as a result of God's original creation, humanity evolved from the primates. And at one point, protohumanity became human. The transition occured when one species of primates became moral and the story of the Garden of Eden is the allegorical account of how this happened. Because it *is* an allegory, there is no need for the Torah to explain in the next chapter where Seth and

Cain found their wives. This is why Jews do not oppose the teaching of the theory of evolution. A 1981 survey in California asked people to choose between the theory of evolution and the biblical version of creation. The results were as follows:

	Creation	Evolution
Protestant	61	29
Roman Catholic	56	32
Jewish	11	82
None	16	69

In Hebrew אדם *adam* is not a name, but the word for mankind or humanity. *Adam* was adopted as a name by later generations, but in the Torah it always refers to mankind. Eve is the slightly erroneous transliteration of the Hebrew word *Khavah* (חוה) which means Life-Giver, referring to the special, unique power of women to give birth to new life. We shall see later that it is due to this special quality that Khavah חוה came to eat of the fruit of the Tree before Adam.

The Torah uses the image of eating to make the concept of internalizing knowledge dramatic and vivid. When you eat, the food enters your body, some of the food's molecules becoming your molecules and functioning as part of your body. The allegorical consumption of the fruit of the Tree of the Knowledge of Good and Evil symbolized humanity's internalization of the values of Good and Evil.

Animals can be taught to behave in ways their owners consider proper or convenient; but these are externalized behavioral patterns taught by conditioning with rewards and punishment. Animals do not understand *why* they do what they are taught. However, adam (אדם) — humanity — is rational, capable of understanding, and spiritual, capable of intuitively experiencing the divine aspect of moral behavior.

The references to the fruit of the Tree of the Knowledge of Good and Evil are the strongest evidence that the Garden of Eden story is an allegory. Obviously, this is a symbolic tree. There is no tree whose fruit is the Knowledge of Good and Evil. Certainly, no apple gives such knowledge. If you were to take the Torah literally, it would be more plausible to speculate that the fruit of the Tree was a fig because, later, the story specifically states that Adam and Eve covered themselves with fig leaves.

The symbol of the apple was injected into the original allegory due to the misinterpretation (primarily by Christian theologians) that Adam and Eve obtained knowledge of sexual desire when they ate the fruit of the Tree. They subsequently had sexual relations and were ashamed because they knew sexual relations were sinful. This misinterpretation was created by the long standing hatred of sex fostered by many religious teachings. That tradition, based on the false assumption that sexual lust leads to sin, still darkens the lives of hundreds of thousands, perhaps millions, of people who are plagued by feelings of guilt and shame over normal sexual activities.

The idea that the fruit of the Tree symbolizes sexual desire and lust is denied by the Torah itself, which states clearly that the fruit of the Tree represents the Knowledge of Good and Evil. Jewish tradition, and the Talmud, hold that Adam and Eve had sexual relations prior to their eating the fruit of the Tree. This conclusion is derived from the statement at the end of Chapter II that a man shall leave his father and mother and cleave unto his wife and they shall be one flesh. Furthermore, it is logical to assume mankind would not need special knowledge to have sexual relations if they were living in a state of nature in the Garden of Eden. They would have had sexual relations by instinct, as all the other animals do.

The true meaning of the Garden of Eden allegory tells us that humanity originally could be compared to infants who lack moral knowledge of right and wrong. As the years go by and the children grow, they begin to understand right from wrong. At length, they internalize the Knowledge of Good and Evil; they acquire a sense of morality. Before the fruit of the Tree of the Knowledge of Good and Evil was consumed, humanity was in the amoral state of nature. Although people could disobey God's commandments, they could not sin. God did not punish humanity for disobedience, because God did not hold humanity responsible for its acts, just as we would not hold babies responsible for their acts.

The perspective of the second description of creation is, as we have noted, primarily psychological and subjective. We must keep this in mind when analyzing the meaning of the serpent in the allegory. God tells Adam that he and Eve may not consume the fruit of the Tree of the Knowledge of Good and Evil. Adam tells Eve that she may not eat the fruit. He also tells her she may not even touch the Tree, adding the extra prohibition, presumably, on the grounds that what she cannot touch, she cannot eat.

This is an example of arrogance. Apparently, Adam, the man, did not regard woman as capable of following one commandment without the restraining influence of a second commandment. His arrogance thwarted his ultimate goal. According to the rabbis, the Serpent was able to convince Eve that she should eat of the Tree by pushing her against it. When she touched the Tree and saw she did not die as Adam said she would, she then assumed both restrictions which Adam had given her in God's name were false.

This is a paradigm for what often happens when parents place precautionary prohibitions on their children in an attempt to secure obedience. The children, recognizing the fallacy and inherent dishonesty in the extra prohibition, lose confidence in all their parents' decisions. The result is equally tragic when the children obey the extraneous prohibition because they are then robbed of the opportunity to develop their own moral strength. Thus parents who violently oppose the use of pot on the grounds that it is the first step to uppers, downers and heroin would do better to reject, by their own example, all mood-affecting drugs, including alcohol, on the grounds they are a cop-out from life.

Note that in the Torah, when the Serpent talks to Eve, he does not lie to her. He says, "You will not die if you eat of it." Earlier, God had told Adam, "On the day you eat of it, you will die." In fact, however, Adam and Eve did not die on the day they ate of it, nor did they die until many, many years afterward, when, finally they died of old age.

Did God then lie to Adam? The clue to the meaning in this difficult passage lies in the Serpent's statement, "For God knows that on the day you do eat of it, your eyes shall be open and you shall be as God, knowing good and evil." When you develop sufficient intelligence to make conscious moral choices, you are also able to contemplate your future death. Animals and infants, living in a state of nature, are unaware that their destiny is to die. The same intellectual capacity which enables humanity to be moral, forces us to anticipate that destiny. It is heavy knowledge. We see mankind trying to cope with it in a profusion of burial customs, and often in other less dignified ways. And this knowledge of impending death was what God meant when He said that "on the day you eat of it, you will die."

"And when the woman saw that the Tree was good for food, and it was a delight to the eyes, and that the Tree was to be desired to make one wise, she took of the fruit and did eat." (III:6) Thus Eve, *Khavah* (חוה) gained the Knowledge of Good and Evil. After *she* gained the Knowledge of Good and Evil, she gave it to Adam and he also ate. It is important to recognize that the woman took the fruit, not because she was curious like a baby, but because she desired to be wise. She wished to become like God. The fruit of the Tree of Good and Evil, moral knowledge, is, as we have discussed, the essential difference between man and the other animals. Animals cannot be held responsible in a moral sense for their actions. Animals have physical attributes, but they lack knowledge of morality. God has moral knowledge but no physical attributes. Humans, alone in this world, are both like animals and like God. They are physical beings possessing moral knowledge.

Nevertheless, according to the story, when man consumed the fruit, it was not with the same motivation as the woman had. So man cannot receive the same credit for bringing mankind into the civilized state of law, social responsibility, and morality. Thus, the Torah teaches that woman has been the mother of morality and civilization. Children's attachment to a parent they want to please, is the ground without which the gradual switch from outside control to self control does not occur.

Psychiatrists now realize that it is nearly impossible to "give" someone a conscience in later life. During the first few years of life, babies learn to restrain their impulses through interaction with their mother's reward and punishment reactions. All of societies' later development depends on the mother's teaching of good and evil during this formative period. Thus, it is truly through Khavah, mother, that all the children of mankind learn morality.

Now we must explain the role of the Serpent. According to the theory of Original Sin, the Serpent is the Devil (or the Sexual Instinct) who lured man to fall from the Grace of God. But we have noted that the Serpent spoke only the truth. He said God knows that on the day that *Adam* (אדם) and *Khavah* (חוה) consume the fruit of morality, they shall become like God. His words must be true because at the end of the chapter, God Himself says, "Man has become as one of us" (III:22).

Without the Serpent's push, humanity might not have acquired moral knowledge and become like God. Using this framework, we see that the Serpent is an agent of Good not Evil. Gematria, the Kabbalistic method of decoding the mysteries of the Torah, (see "The Hidden Code of the Kabbalah" for details), gives the same conclusion we have reached through logic.

The numerical value of the Hebrew word *Na-khash* (נחש) is 358 which is the exact numerical equivalent of the Hebrew word משיח Messiah. Thus the *Na-khash* (נחש) — Serpent — is an annointed Divine agent (see "The coming of the Messianic Age"). But, if this interpretation is correct, why does the Serpent have to suffer by crawling on its belly and eating the dust? And why do men have to work, or women give birth in pain.

The answer to the pain of childbirth is two fold. Since we are self conscious, we anticipate and get tense about things. Part of the pain of childbirth is psychological, and animals are spared this anxiety. But there is a physical reason also. We evolved large brains so we need large skulls, and a baby skull is much bigger relative to its mother's pelvis than any other mammal. So women pay double for mankind's intellectual abilities.

Men work — as opposed to just foraging enough to live on, because they desire more than subsistence, and the excess product allows for civilization. The snake crawls on its belly because we don't like the forces that push us to higher levels of achievement, when they do so against our will. Have you ever tried to give advice to someone who needed it? Even though your intentions are good, and your words filled with wisdom and truth, you will often find that you are resented and condemned just as the serpent was.

We have been thinking a great deal about the symbolism of the Tree of Knowledge of Good and Evil. But there was another symbolic tree in the garden: The Tree of Life (Genesis 2:9). Why didn't Adam eat of the Tree of Life which was not prohibited to him? Adam didn't want Eve to be equal to him. He remembered all the trouble he had with his first wife, Lilith. (See "Lilith: Queen of the Demons"). Since Eve was younger than Adam, he was afraid that if they both ate of the Tree of Life, neither of them would age, and therefore over the centuries he would lose his favorite argument; that he knew best because he was much older and more experienced.

Thus Adam encouraged the woman to eat frequently of the Tree of Life, while he only took a few nibbles. The woman ate of the Tree of Life and retained her youthful vigor and charm. But as the decades went by, she became increasingly frustrated by her failure to conceive. She desperatly wanted to become pregnant and to bear a child. To be a life giver was her very essence. Finally, the woman went for advice to the creature who had the reputation for being the most subtle of all the creatures in the field (Gen. 3:1). The serpent explained that the reason she could not conceive was due to her eating of the fruit of the Tree of Life. Hadn't she noticed that in the area around the Tree of Life there were no little trees growing. The big trees blocked out all the sunlight from reaching the floor of the forest. Since none of the trees died, there was never any opening where the sunlight could come in and nourish a seedling. Unless some of the old trees died, there would never be any room for new trees to grow.

Not only that, but the old trees didn't look very good. Since no one ever pruned them, they kept growing more and more straggly. There was more life in them, but it was of lower quality. The only way for woman to achieve the fertility and creativity which was her desire, the serpent told her, would be to accept the value of death in the scheme of life.

It was then that the serpent encouraged the woman to eat of the Tree of Knowledge of Good and Evil. She did so because she wanted the wisdom to understand both the meaning of birth and creativity, as well as the meaning and function of death, in the scheme of life. This is why she is referred to as the woman all during the story, and only after she has eaten of the fruit of the Knowledge of Good and Evil (Gen. 3:6), and after God has promised her that she will bring forth children (Gen. 3:16) does Adam call her Eve חוה (Gen. 3:20). Thus the verse that follows the statement that they were driven out of the Garden of Eden relates that Eve conceived and bore a child. Once woman has made the choice for birth and death, moral values and responsibilities, God acts to expel mankind from the Garden before Adam can regress by eating greedily of the Tree of Life (Gen. 3:22). God places before the Garden, a flaming sword, to prevent us from trying to eliminate death any time in the future; a warning to those doctors whose efforts to keep patients alive, who should be allowed to die, is a prolonging of death rather than a restoring of health.

To this day the sons of Adam usually prefer to marry women who are younger than they are, and the daughters of Eve say they are younger than they really are. Since Eve ate much more from the Tree of Life than Adam did, women still tend to live longer than men.

The best indication that Eve did eat of the Tree of Life is found in the biblical witness that the early generations of her children lived for 700 to 900 years. As the potency of the fruit of the Tree of Life was dissipated, the ages of her descendants declined: Abraham's father died at the age of 205; Joseph died at the age of 110; and thereafter everyone lived a normal life span. The early chapters of Genesis do not relate the life spans of the women because they exceeded that of the men by such a great amount that it embarrassed later generations.

The Garden of Eden allegory raises another question: Why didn't God give humanity moral knowledge directly instead of arranging events so that *Adam* (אדם) and *Khavah* (חוה) acquired the fruit of moral knowledge from the נחש Serpent? And why did God seemingly punish them for consuming it?

The popular belief that humanity, as symbolized by Adam and Eve, was punished for eating the fruit is the result of a translator's error. In the early translations from the Hebrew the word *Arrur* (ארור) was translated by its usual meaning cursed or banned. More accurately in this context, it implies *restricted* or *constrained*. When we say event A inevitably results in event B, we are alluding to the restriction or contraint meant by the word *Arrur* (ארור). Leaving childhood behind and growing up by internalizing values, limits and inhibitions, restricts or contrains the behavior of the developing individual who must cope with the responsibilities of being an adult. These responsibilities are not a punishment, they are part of the consequences of being an adult. Usually we see our inhibitions, as a punishment from our parents, when we don't like them, and as our own virtues, when we do like them.

The underlying meaning of this part of the allegory is that every man and woman (as symbolized by *Adam* and *Khavah*) begins life as an infant living in a state of dependency (the Garden of Eden) in which everything is provided by the parents. As dependents, under the authority of their parents, infants encounter a series of commandments. They are told not to touch dangerous objects, not to eat dirty and unwholesome substances, not to go naked among strangers and so forth. Infants are totally dependent. Yet they must explore, challenge, suffer, and learn enough to mature and realize their own unique souls.

The Serpent is this instinct of growth. It is this instinct (the Serpent), that urges us to seek out new experiences, which in time leads us to internalize moral values. Towards the end of this passage, children reach a point, as they struggle to become adults, where a series of conflicts develop between them and their parents, who still see them as children and who wish to shield them from pain. Although parents want their children to become mature, responsible individuals, they hesitate to give them freedom, and its concomitant consequences, of rising or falling with that freedom. This is symbolized by the unwillingness of God, the Parent-Creator, to give mankind moral knowledge directly — "but of the fruit of the Tree of Knowledge of Good and Evil you shall not eat." The allegory points out a psychological truth: *it is impossible for someone, even God, to give anyone else either freedom or responsibility.* Everyone must struggle to make themselves free and responsible..

Without the Serpent, humanity would have remained in the Garden of Eden. In other words, people generally prefer security (the Garden) to freedom and independence. Yet we want our independence, if we can have it easily and without pain. We cannot have both. This ambivalence is reflected in the role of the Serpent in introducing the possibility of humanity's becoming like God. But all growth is change; all change is unstable and frequently uncomfortable; and often accompanied by fears of failure. Human beings no longer are able to avoid growth and change because we have left the Garden. Animal behavior changes little from generation to generation. Human beings can change their life styles markedly in a generation or less.

And each of us does struggle, even though at times we seem to be struggling against the parents we love, because the instinct for growth, for independence, for freedom and maturity (represented by the Serpent, which the Torah describes as clever) is the inner core of every normal human being. Once the struggle for independence is complete, parents and children become copartners in the business of life and work together, although, very few parents are capable of seeing their children as completely independent of them.

With extraordinary psychological insight and pith, the Torah, in this second account of creation, has described and given its sanction to the process of human and individual moral development. The consequence — not the punishment — of being an adult is that the individual provides for himself. After marriage and parenthood, a man and woman provide for the needs of their children as well and this, too, is a consequence, not a punishment. A mother feels responsible for the nourishment, comfort, and safety of her baby. However much she loves and wants to care for her child, the doing of it *is* labor and toil, and a decided limitation on her activities. And while the mother nurses and looks after their baby, the father works to supply the family with food, shelter, clothing, and the other necessities of life. The agricultural image used by the Torah is to till the soil by the sweat of your brow.

Some of the patterns of earning a living have changed over the years, and currently some of the patterns of how couples divide up their parental tasks are changing, but the main outline remains the same as it was when the Torah was written down for the first time: *Adam* and *Khavah* — man and woman — become parents and assume the responsibility for a family. Any new parents will tell you that it is difficult, even painful, at times to be parents. Nevertheless, the independence and the responsibilities of being the parent rather than the child are among the greatest glories, and the greatest sources of satisfaction for men and women.

There is another mystery hidden in one of the comments at the end of this chapter. When God says, "Behold man has become as one of us, to know Good and Evil," what is meant by "one of us?" Some say God is addressing the angels, and referring to the fact that like all of the inhabitants of the spiritual-intellectual realm, mankind has acquired moral knowledge. Others say God is using the royal "us" to refer to Himself. I propose a new explanation.

Our earth is one of nine planets circling our sun. Our sun is one of two hundred billion stars in our galaxy. Our sun is an average star. Many stars are much larger, and many are much smaller than our sun. Our galaxy is also average and there are thousands of millions of other galaxies like our own in the universe. As we mentioned in the first part of this chapter most astronomers believe that the same process that formed the stars — the condensation of gases created from the cosmic explosion which started the universe — also formed the planets.

It would not be surprising if stars with planetary systems are quite common. It is probable that the majority of stars in the various galaxies have planetary systems. If only one out of ten in fact *do* have planets, and if only one out of ten thousand of the planets was the necessary distance from its sun, and the necessary temperature, and of the appropriate chemical composition so that life, as we understand it, could develop, there must be tens of thousands of planets that have some form of life among the two hundred billion stars in our galaxy (see "Intelligent Life in Outer Space").

It took several billion years for intelligent life to develop on earth, and it is only in the last ten to fifty thousand years that man, a creature capable of knowing good and evil, arose. It would be presumptuous and egotistical to believe that our planet was the first of all the thousands of planets with life to evolve intelligent beings. It is more logical to assume that, since ours is an average star and, most likely an average planet, our evolutionary timetable — the rate at which evolutionary events culminating in intelligent life developed — compared with the timetable of other planets — is also average. The chances seem great that hundreds of other planets in our own galaxy, and thousands and thousands of planets throughout the universe, are ahead of us in the evolutionary scheme.

It is plausible to assume that intelligent life and moral creatures developed elsewhere, ten thousand, or perhaps a hundred thousand years prior to their development on earth. Therefore, when in the Torah, God says that man has become like one of us, the Torah is hinting at the reality, understandable to us only in terms of recent astronomical theory, that there are other creatures which, like man, combine both the physical properties that result from evolution, with the spiritual insight of moral judgment derived from God's influence. When mankind consumed the fruit of the Tree of the Knowledge of Good and Evil we joined the ranks of creatures throughout the universe who have also become like God.

Of course, physically, all these creatures must differ tremendously, their forms and attributes would be shaped by the size, and the conditions of the planets upon which they live. But they are all united in that the God who pervades the entire universe, in all of its hundreds of millions of galaxies, has shared with them the experience of the wisdom of Good and Evil.

The possibility that intelligent life does exist in the universe beyond our own planet is accepted and understood today by growing numbers of people. A Gallup poll taken in 1966 indicated that thirty-four percent of the population of the United States believes that there is intelligent life on other planets. By 1973 the percentage had risen to forty-six percent. Few, if any of these people see the relationship between the Biblical statement, and their views on extraterrestrial life. But in a few decades all will see it.

Some time after 1997, I believe we will have contact with intelligent, moral creatures from outer space. There are some who believe our planet has already been visited by intelligent creatures from outer space, pointing out that historical records, including those of the Torah, make obscure references to these visits. The rabbis spoke of the descent of the Chariot, referring to the first Chapter of Ezekiel, especially verses four through twenty-seven, as well as the tenth Chapter, especially verses six through twenty-two. But I may write no more of this for the Talmud says that "The work of Creation (Genesis Chapter I, II, and III) may not be expounded in the presence of two, nor may the work of the Chariot be expounded in the presence of even one, unless he is a sage, and can follow with his own understanding."

The needs of the day have persuaded me to break the first part of this proscription, but the work of the Chariot is a much more difficult and dangerous doctrine, and may not be expounded in public. He who would understand must first find and win the confidence of a Hassidic rabbi in Philadelphia, whose name is Zalman Schacter.

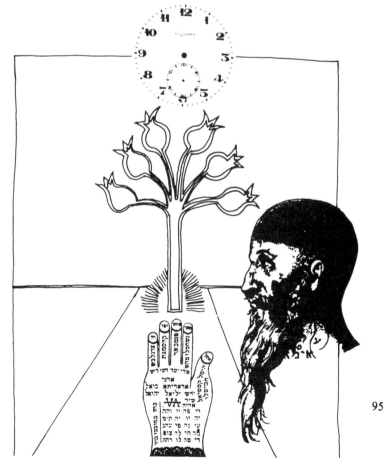

THE SHEKINAH

For centuries the Jews have called God, She, when talking about the שכינה Shekinah, the female presence of Divinity.

Actually, God is One, formless and shapeless, neither male nor female. But the Bible used human images in talking about God to suggest productive human relationships with God. The Torah speaks of God as a father to His people, or as a king who rules over His people. This implies that when we trust, respect and obey Him, take pride in and do our duty toward God, He will protect, lead, sustain and inspire us. It's up to us. These relationships are open to us, but we must fulfill our part by loving God, by being faithful and by trusting Him. Father and king are not exact terms. They are the words we use for evoking close, functional feeling relationships to Deity.

To express God's sexlessness more exactly, we should refer to God as It. The gain in precision, however, would steal from function. Finite, emotional human beings cannot easily work up devotion to an impersonal force. Most people have a deeper relationship to their family dog than to an abstract concept of God. Today, in a world increasingly controlled by impersonal institutions and organizations, we need to think of God in strongly personal terms. We are continually jarred by the indifference of schools, businesses, and governments to us as individuals. Thinking of the Deity in non-personal terms would only further depersonalize us and increase that sense of lost ties to God that already burdens our time.

Not only do we need to retain the personal images of God found in the Torah, but we can benefit from the rich emotional associations evoked by an image of God introduced in the Talmud and developed by the Kabbalists-God viewed as a feminine principle, the Shekinah שכינה. Historically, the preponderance of images stressing masculine relationships probably resulted from male dominance of society, and the relative absence of women's impact outside the home. After all, the feelings aroused by feminine relationships, by the image of mother or wife, are just as strong, perhaps stronger, than many of the masculine images used to suggest God.

The images centering around the Shekinah range all the way from such concrete terms as *queen, princess,* or *great lady* to a *numinous presence* preferred by those who wish to temper their imagery with a bit of rationalism. There are half a dozen different references to bringing a convert to Judaism "under the wings of the Shekinah". Here the words suggest a mother bird tucking her newborns under her wings, and giving them warmth and protection. This feeling would not have been conveyed by a masculine image of God.

As with the masculine images, the images of the Shekinah do not imply form, but they do imply very special and distinct qualities. She represents a distinct and important perspective of God. The Shekinah is not God, the Creator of heaven and earth, nor is She the God of Justice and Revelation, or the God of historic redemption. She is God, our indwelling awareness of the Superpersonal, the transcendant aspect of the Divine in our lives.

The God of Nature is a universal force; the God of Justice rests on abstract principles; the God of Redemption relates to society as a whole; but the Shekinah rests upon individual human beings when they act lovingly, with kindness and joy. When She touches people's lives, her Presence can be felt. She is warm and comfortable and personable. She has been called the Divine Presence, an awareness of spirituality.

A young mother recalls that during natural childbirth, at that moment of ecstacy and joy when her child was emerging, she felt "that there was another Being" with her, not the doctors or the nurses, but a Presence. Similarly, a son, visiting his dying father, felt there was a Presence in the room with them. The Shekinah makes us aware that there is another dimension beyond the mundane. We can think logically about the Ein Sof, (the Infinate One) but the Shekinah can only be experienced.

The Kabbalists identified the Divine Presence that dwells closest to us with the tenth and final stage of the Sefirot, the Sefirah called Malkut. Malkut (מלכות) is the Divine emanation which brought the physical universe into being. It is, therfore, the closest link, the bridge, between the finite world and the אין סוף Ein Sof, the Infinite One. Those who have come to think of God as remote can use this perspective to reach out for the Divine Presence that can touch our lives and be sensed. How, then, can we reach out and find the Divine Presence?.

What is unique about the Shekinah is that She may be wooed. Evil and coldness drive her away, but goodness brings Her close. When ten people sit together and discuss words of the Torah, or even when people study Torah alone, the Shekinah rests upon them. Jews going into prayer, wrapped in their prayer shawls, are wrapped round in the Shekinah, for the mystics say that She hovers in the fringes (tsitsit) of the shawl.

She cannot be wooed by those who are idle or sad or frivolous, but only by those who are joyful, and who work hard to make life good for those around them. Welcoming an elderly person in your midst is said to be equivalent to welcoming the Shekinah Herself. She hovers over the bed of a sick person who is visited by someone. She is drawn to innocent joy. When the Jews went into exile, the Shekinah did not leave with the religious leaders, instead She accompanied the school children. In the kibbutz of Israel where people joyously work together for a common goal Her Presence has been felt also.

She is more responsive to sincere devotion than to the letter of the law. She is not reported as being wooed by the strict observance of the Sabbath, or the laws of Kosher food. Indeed it is stated that She dwells among Israel even if they are ritually impure.

The Shekinah cannot, however, tolerate wrong doing. Ritual impurity — which results from touching a corpse, or menstruating, or having a nocturnal emission — is an absence of purity rather than a cruel or immoral act. Unchastity causes the Shekinah to depart. Those who mock, the hypocrits, the slanders, and the liars cannot see Her at all. But when people gather together in loving kindness and joy, She descends and dwells among them.

The Divine energy which sustains the created universe radiates through the Shekinah. Everything that happens to Israel is reflected upon Her. She goes into exile as we do, suffers as we suffer, and is redeemed as we are redeemed. The Shekinah is the first goal of those who seek God.

Just as an evil person repels Her, so too does a period of evil, such as the days of Nazi Germany. In times of great evil, the Shekinah is remote, forcing people to struggle harder in order to experience Her, but in times of great goodness, She can be felt with less effort. After the Holocaust, when the State of Israel was created, the Shekinah began to return to humanity. The reunification of the holy city of Jerusalem in 1967 brought the Shekinah even closer. This nearness is reflected in the religious revivals occuring all over America, many of which began in, and shortly after 1967. The cumulative effect of many people's behavior on the Shekinah, is the reason the frequency of mystical experiences among a people waxes and wanes with the goodness within society.

During the middle ages there were those who sought and achieved mystical experiences although they also were engaging in vicious wrongdoing, such as the slaughter of their fellow humans. The mystical experiences of such people were demonic. The possibility of being possessed by demonic mystical experiences lies behind the warnings in this book, and the many restrictions that have been placed on the study of the Kabbalah in the past. To prevent demonic experiences, the practice of meditation should always be accompanied by scrupulous attention to performing mitzvot. A Divine mystical experience is known by its effect. The closer we reach to the Shekinah, the more love and concern we feel for our fellow human beings, and the rest of God's creation.

The safest and most effective way to reach out to the Shekinah is through love. This concept, that the Shekinah can be found by individuals who are committed to deep emotional relationships, has a great deal to offer our age of self-actualization and supercool.

The joy that comes from the sexual expression of love by a husband and wife, make it the easiest and most accessible method of discovering how to reach the Shekinah through love. People who do not feel God's Presence in history, in philosophy, in nature, or even in their relationship to their family and friends, often are able to experience the nearness of the Shekinah through the sense of wonder they feel during lovemaking.

There is a statement in the Talmud that the Shekinah rests between a man and his wife if they are worthy. Remember, the Kabbalists identified the Shekinah with the tenth Sefirah, Malkut. The next stage upward toward the Divine in that system is the ninth Sefirah, יסוד Yesod, one of the masculine principles. When superimposed on אדם הקדמון Adam Hakadmon, the prototype human (see "The Tree of Life"), Yesod occupies the region of the penis. Thus, the ninth Sefirah, generates the tenth which in turn brings forth the physical universe; the sexual energy of human love, within marital sanctity, resonates with the interaction between יסוד Yesod and מלכות Malkut.

Currently, sex is not regarded as a holy act, but is viewed either as a necessary discharge of energy, as trivial fun, or an act of gamesmanship. (See "Sex and Divine Intercourse in the Zohar"). The pick-up, the conquest, the affair, are elements of power; asserting our ego, fulfilling our needs, achieving success. A marital commitment of deep love involves going beyond the self to the other, desiring to please the other, desiring the good of the other, enjoying the giving as well as the receiving, accepting the other's personality, respecting the other's dignity, and being happy just by being with the other. In lovemaking within such a marriage, the lovers feel a sense of awe that they are loved by someone so wonderful. They feel not fully worthy of their lover. They feel grateful that their mate puts up with all their weaknesses, fears, and inabilities.

Many who have actually experienced the Shekinah at those times have not been trained to recognize the Divine Presence, and cannot explain even

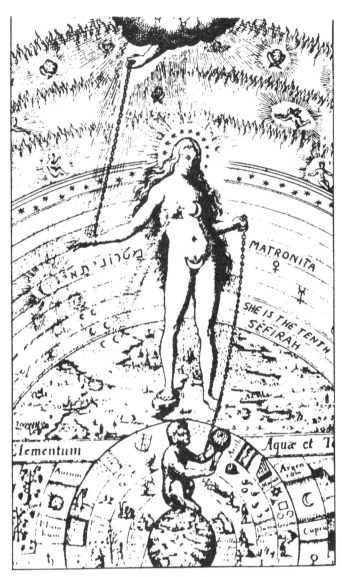

By de Bry for
Robert Fludd,
Collectio Operum
Oppenheim,
1617.

to themselves what they feel. It is the sense that the other is greater than the self that parallels the religious experience of a relationship with God, the Greatest of all others. At the time of lovemaking, if one feels oneself merging into the other, if one feels like thanking God for having such a lover, who is so much more than you deserve, if one finds amazement in having been blessed by the other's love, one has been touched by the transcendance of the Divine.

Such experiences are few in a society which emphasizes self-fulfillment, individual accomplishment, and ego-gratification. Yet generations of sensitive individuals agree that love *is* a form of bondage. But with love the acceptance of responsibility and commitment is voluntary. True lovers bind each to the other, subsuming the self, each in effect being the servant of the other, eager to please, to give, and even to obey. Much of the time true lovers desire doing what the other commands, rather than exercise their own will power.

Thus, the rabbis say that those who fulfill the mitzvot because they are commanded, are on a higher level than those who do them because they want to, or who think the rules are for their own good. This sounds strange because we usually consider a person who volunteers to be superior to the person who only works when obliged to. Yet the dynamics of love are such that the voluntary offering still contains something of one's ego, whereas the offering that is made because the lover commanded it, is made for the other rather than the self. Hence it is the purer offering.

The Hebrew root *eved* has three distinct meanings: to work, to serve, and to worship. All three of these meanings apply to marriage. The husband *works* for the wife, usually supporting her financially while she cares for their children, and contributing physical effort to building their life together. The husband *serves* his wife by attempting to meet her psychological and emotional needs as well as her material needs. And, on a spiritual intellectual level, the husband *worships* his wife as a means of approaching the Divine Presence.

The husband feels the Shekinah is present in him due to his wife, and his love for her, and her love for him. The wife, too, experiences the awe of sensing the nearness of the Divine Presence. This awareness, one of the most magnificent aspects of married life, makes their home a sanctuary, a house of holiness. Their bed is a sacred spot, and the blessing they derive from each other is not limited to the five senses of the human animal, but that other dimension that opens up to us through the Shekinah.

Approaching the Shekinah through marriage brings mysticism into the couple's daily lives. Although approaching the Shekinah may usefully begin with marriage, it should not be limited to marriage. Having learned how to reach out to the Divine Presence through mutual joy and powerful commitment, the couple should expand those feelings to include their children, and other members of their family, their friends, and their community. Slowly, all their relationships deepen and become more nourishing, both in what they give and what they receive. At the same time their attitude and feelings toward their daily activities change. Because they feel work is a service, and their recreation an expression of their joy in those they love, even seemingly unimportant chores and outings begin to glow with importance and satisfaction.

Of course, for this couple as for any other, life's nuisances, frustrations, griefs, anger, and fears continue. But those who have learned to draw the Shekinah close to them feel, underneath the surface churning of daily troubles, a deep strong current of joy and thanksgiving to be part of God's creation.

This was the secret of the ancient Jewish mystics. They wore no special clothing. They worked at few special tasks. They lived in no segregated communities. If they meditated or prayed more than their neighbors, not many knew it. They certainly did not need to act conspicuously pious, or righteous, or even important. When they were noticeable at all, it was because people felt special being around them. In part it stemmed from their ability to draw others into the circle of their spirituality, but most important of all, it came from Her, the Shekinah, who dwelt upon them.

LILITH, QUEEN OF THE DEMONS

Probably, you were taught the first woman was Eve who was made after Adam's creation from one of his ribs, but chapter one of Genesis reads, "God created mankind, male and female, created He them". This passage states God created the male and female of our species simultaneously. Only the second account of creation (see "The Secrets of Creation") tells the popular story that Adam was created in solitary splendor, and Eve was created thereafter... for the purpose of relieving Adam's loneliness.

If God created a woman at the same time He made Adam, while Eve's creation came later, who was that first female and what happened to her?

A number of legends attempt to answer that question. One of the most detailed is found in a text called the *Alphabeth of Ben Sira*. This manuscript, written between the fifth and eighth centuries of the common era, tells us that Adam's first wife was Lilith. She was not only the first woman but the prototype of liberated women everywhere. The legend doesn't state whether she was once fond of Adam, but it does describe their passionate quarrel over the arrangements of their sexual relationship.

Pointing out that she had been created simultaneously as Adam's partner, and should be treated with equal dignity, Lilith insisted that she should not always have to be underneath Adam when they were making love.

Perhaps she would have preferred always to be above Adam, but the legend indicates that she was willing to negotiate, suggesting the possibility of sharing the onus of the supine position. We may assume that in those days of beginnings, when all was new and little tried, more subtle compromises of this conflict had yet to be discovered. At any event, the legend tells us that Lilith's sense of dignity and independence forced her to refuse to go beyond an equal sharing of the burden. She wanted to be on top too.

Adam, the true progenitor of all male chauvenist pigs, *adam*antly refused to serve under Lilith.

Under the conditions of that refusal, Lilith refused to have sexual relations with Adam.

A stalemate ensued.

If there had been rabbis in those days, they might have found an equitable solution to this impasse. But, alas, there were none. Adam's and Lilith's inability to relate to each other brought forth frustration. Not just frustration for Adam and Lilith, but a frustration of the entire biological destiny of the human species.

Finding their positions irreconcilable. Lilith stamped off in a huff to live on the beach of the Red Sea's Gulf of Aqaba.

Finding himself quite lonely and very desirous, Adam called on his Maker for help in this, his first major crisis. It was clear that something would have to be done if humanity were to survive its first generation. So, the Lord sent three messengers — Sanoi, Sansanoi, and Smengalef — to act as marriage counselors.

They entreated Lilith to return to Adam.

She refused.

They tried to pressure her into returning to Adam.

Lilith would not budge. She would not lay down her pride.

They warned her if she did not yield to Adam's demands, she would be replaced by a more docile and willing creature, one who could satisfy her sense of dignity by bearing and raising children, and would be happy to accept the subordinate position.

Lilith retorted with threats of her own, swearing to take vengeance on the lives of any such women, and on their children.

Lilith remained apart from Adam. So God made Eve from Adam's body.

Transformed by her jealous rage into a demon, Lilith began attacking women, especially at the time of childbirth, and strangling newly born infants as well as babies in the first few months of life.

That is the legend from the *Alphabeth of Ben Sira,* but the tradition of Lilith's existence is older than the manuscript. It antedates Jewish history. A female demon named Lilith can be traced back to Babylonian times, and still earlier to Sumerian mythology, which refers to a female spirit by the name of Lilitu who preyed on women in childbirth and the babes they bore. A winged female demon who strangles children is mentioned on a Hebrew or Cannanite inscription dating from the seventh or eighth century, BCE which was found in northern Syria.

There were demons in most cultures who brought death to mother and child at the moment of birth, before modern medicine exorcised the demons by making childbirth relatively safe and painless. Ignorance and suffering caused by disease have a demonic influence on people's lives, so that it is not surprising that they take on terrible shapes in human imagination.

The Bible generally ignored or played down the importance of demons, mentioning Lilith only once. In the prophet Isaiah (34:14) Lilith is referred to as one of the creatures who will lay waste to the land on the Day of Vengeance. The Talmud, especially the Babylonian Talmud, mentions Lilith several times. However, her personality took shape primarily during the six centuries between the writing down of the Talmud and the writing down of the Zohar.

As her personality developed, so did the scope of her malevolent activities. She became a seducer of men, leading her conquests to destruction. According to the Talmud, a man who sleeps in a house alone, is vulnerable to attack by Lilith. The obvious moral: Men, do not sleep in a house alone. The feeling in the Jewish community that it is not respectable to be single over thirty may have sprung from the danger of being snared by Lilith.

During the Middle Ages, one of the standard ways to protect newly born infants and their mothers from Lilith's vengeance was to give them amulets inscribed with the names of the three messengers — Sanoi, Sansanoi, and Smengalef, and either Psalm 121 or 126. Some amulets were also engraved with Lilith bound in chains.

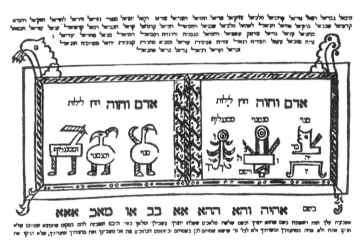

An amulet with the names of Sanoi, Sansonoi, and Smengalef, used to protect a women during childbirth, from the Kabbalistic Book of Raziel.

Until the end of the eighteenth century approximately 20 to 30 percent of all newborn infants died within a few months of their birth. It was a lucky mother who did not lose at least one or two infants. In an age when medical technology was yet to be, these amulets served to reduce the pregnant mother's fears, if they did nothing else.

As modern hygenic practice and medical skills sharply cut the infant mortality rate in the nineteenth century, fear of Lilith began to decline. By the beginning of the twentieth century, the terrifying figure of Lilith had dwindled to a folk myth when she was remembered at all. But today Lilith has returned, becoming a symbol of potent positive and negative female forces at work.

Most people are surprised by the notion that a demon can use its power for good. We tend to think of demons as totally sinful and malign agents of the Christian devil. Judaism, of course, does not believe that there is a powerful and independent force of evil challenging God's rule. The Jewish concept of שטן Satan is more in the image of a prosecuting attorney who calls our attention to wrongdoing, whether we wish to see it or not, rather than a force for creating evil. The difference between Satan and the devil is the difference between General Motors's view of Ralph Nader, and the consumer movement's view.

The consumer movement knows that Nader did not create the Corvair's dangerous characteristics but only called our attention to them. However, by drawing attention to their wrongdoing, he seems to be the very embodiment of the devil to G.M. management. As power figures Jewish demons have constructive aspects as well as destructive ones. Today, the spirit of Lilith in both aspects of her nature is alive and active.

The woman's liberation movement represents the positive side of Lilith — creative, self-assertive, independent, willing to share, but only as an equal partner. There is a possibility that the woman's movement will endanger the family by its apparent denigration of motherhood and child care. To a large extent, the success of the woman's movement in restructuring family roles in ways that are both more adaptive to the needs of our own times, and yet continue to be nourishing for all the members of the family, depends upon how the sons of Adam react to the demands to the daughters of Lilith.

While the woman's movement can be seen as an aspect of Lilith's positive nature, the alienation of Jewish youth and its assimilation into other religions or groups reflects her destructive side.

Traditionally, Lilith's ability to materialize and lead a nice Jewish boy to destruction came from her identification with the Queen of Sheba, the non-Jewish beauty who visited and tempted King Solomon. Jews and Arabs alike claimed this particular Queen of Sheba was actually a Jinn, a dangerous human-demon hybrid. Folk history reports the riddles she posed to Solomon in her attempt to capture his interest and seduce him, were the same ones she had used on Adam when she was attempting to inviegle him into assuming the subordinate position in the marriage bed.

Those who are mystically inclined, can deduce from this background why so many Jewish parents react negatively to the prospect of their son marrying a non-Jewish girl. Of course, even the most traditional parents don't believe non-Jewish women are possessed by the Lilith demon. Unfortunately even without malign intent, a gentile wife, through her failure to participate in Jewish religious and cultural activities, effectively lures her spouse away from the traditions of his people.

Parents may not belong to a synagogue or attend services regularly; they may have lost much of their owen faith; still they will fear the consequences of such a marriage. They are afraid their grandchildren will grow up ignorant of Jewish traditions and without any feelings of loyalty to the Jewish people. They fear the chain of tradition, which goes back 120 generations to Mount Sinai, will be broken.

The Jewish people are one of mankind's endangered species. Our visible enemies are the Russians and the Arabs, but our invisible enemy is the growing practice of young Jewish men marrying non-Jews. These mixed marriages fulfill the curse of Lilith because the children of those unions are, in 80% of the cases, lost to the Jewish community. They are not given a Jewish education and they usually think of themselves as "half Jewish" or "nothing". Their parents without intending it are helping complete Hitler's work.

Of course the survival of the Jewish people is ultimately the result of the Covenant between God and Israel. However, it is up to us to endeavor in every way possible to ensure the continuity of the Jewish tradition and therefore the identity of the Jewish people. If the Jewish birthrate was well above the replacement rate the effect of mixed marriage would not be as devastating as it is. Unfortunately, the Jewish birthrate is well below average, and is in fact below the net reproductive rate. Therefore, if 3 out of 4 children who are born to Jewish-Gentile marriages are not raised as Jews, and these marriages make up some 30% or more of all marriages involving Jews, it is clear that each generation will suffer a loss of anywhere from 10 to 20% of the Jewish community.

It is ironic that many people who worry about the possible extinction of a species of bird, animal, or even insect, do not seem to worry about the potential demise of an ethnic or cultural group of human beings. Are not the varieties of human beings just as important as the varieties of birds or butterflies? In truth, human variety is even more impurtant, since it is the result of spiritual/cultural factors and not simply natural selection. Jews are not the only endangered species among homo sapiens. Every small people and nation needs to preserve its unique culture, and the large expanding groups need to help the minorities to grow while they cut back.

The solution to both the declining Jewish population as well as the increasing incidence of mixed marriage is the adoption by the non-Jewish spouse of Judaism. If the Jewish community reaches out to the world and welcomes into the family of Israel all those who love a Jew, encouraging them to love the Jewish people and its traditions, Lilith will be converted from a frustrated destroyer into a builder of a home where her power can be used to strengthen the Jewish people. This approach is the most effective amulet of all against the evil of the Lilith demon.

All that I have written above also applies to non-Jewish men who marry Jewish women. In the past, fear of circumscion kept many males from converting, but today non-Jewish men in increasing numbers are adding to the strength of the Jewish people. Formal conversion is not so essential for a man as it is for a women because orthodox Jewish law recognizes the children of a non-Jewish man married to a Jewish women as being Jewish. But if he wishes to truely protect his wife and children from anti-semitism and assimilation he should become Jewish.

בָּרוּךְ אַתָּה, יְיָ אֱלֹהֵינוּ, מֶלֶךְ הָעוֹלָם, אֲשֶׁר קִדְּשָׁנוּ בְּמִצְוֹתָיו וְצִוָּנוּ עַל אַהֲבַת גֵּרִים.

Blessed are you Adonai our God Ruler of the universe who has santified us by his Mitsvot and commanded us to love converts.

HELL NO, WE WON'T GO

Do you believe that God created a place of eternal punishment? Most Christians do; 70% of Catholics and 68% of Protestants according to a Gallup poll. Only 4% of the Jews polled believed in hell. That's not very many, actually fewer than those who said they had no religion at all.

Usually Christians are quite surprised to learn that not only do Jews not believe in hell, but very few Jews believe in heaven either. The same poll noted that only 20% of the Jews agree with the 90% of all Protestants and Catholics who believe in heaven.

The gap between Jews and Christians seems to be growing with the passage of time. A survey of over 1800 youth (18-28) taken in 1935 found that 78% of Catholics believed in a reward or punishment after death compared to 44% of Protestants. But the figure for Jews was only 6%. Most Jewish youth felt that we just don't know enough to say (38%), or that you live on in the influence you had on the lives of others, especially your children (23%), or that after death there is nothing (27% compared to 4% of Protestants and 3% of Catholics). The famous German Philosopher, Immanual Kant, denied that Biblical Judaism was a religion at all, "since no religion can be conceived of which involves no belief in a future life. Judaism, which taken in all it's purity is seen to lack this belief, is not a religious faith at all". Of course, this simply illustrates the very limited or prejudicial thinking of some Philosophers.

Jewish teaching about life after death has varied from age to age. The Bible refers to some kind of an after-life but only very briefly and vaguely. The Rabbinic sages did teach that there is a reward and punishment in store for each individual according to his or her manner of living on earth. The Kabbalah teaches that souls undergo reincarnation. This teaching became wide spread during the 16-18th centuries, especially among the Hassidim. The majority of modern Jews are closer to the Biblical teachings, but all the various positions can be found among Rabbis today.

Christians frequently wonder why Jews try to do good if they do not expect a reward or punishment in their after-life. Jews, in turn, find it hard to understand why that is so important to Christians. Judaism teaches that the reason for doing the Mitzvah, is the Mitzvah itself.

Judaism places the primary emphasis upon life in this world. Although there have been times when belief in an after-life was an important part of the Jewish consciousness, it never assumed the significance (either in the folk or in the philosophical mind) that it did in Christianity.

A Gallup poll shows this clearly. People were asked, "Which do you think you should be most serious about — trying to live comfortably, or preparing for a life after death?" 46% of Catholics, 62% of Baptists, 50% of Methodists, 47% of 'Lutherans and 00% of Jews said. "Prepare for life after death", Whether they were conscious of it or not, the Jews were simply articulating the teaching of the Talmud that states, "Better one hour of repentance and good deeds in this world, than the whole of the life in the world to come".

The Jewish Bible speaks neither of heaven or hell. It does on a few occasions refer to the existance that follows death as Sheol. The root meaning of the Hebrew word, שאול Sheol, comes from the verb Sha'al which means to question, ask or request. It is possible that the use of this word is due to the fact that while everyone asks about what happens after death, nobody really knows, so the after-life remains an open question. In the Bible, Sheol seems to be the place, or the dimension of existence, where the spirits of the departed continue their existence. Occasionally Sheol seems to refer to the actual grave itself.

In Biblical times Jewish thought placed primary emphasis on this world, and upon mankinds obligations to God and to our fellow humans in this life. The number of references to Sheol or to any of it's synonyms, and the number of passages devoted to the question of life after death or the soul's reward or punishment, does not take up even one half of one percent of the pages in the Hebrew Bible.

Interest in life after death and the development of theories concerning it occurred primarily at the very end of the Biblical period, and during the early Rabbinic period. During the Babylonian exile, particularly when the Jews had become part of the Persian Empire, they came in contact with ideas from the Zoroasterian religion, which places a great deal of emphasis on a dualistic concept of deity: a good God's eternal war with a bad God, both of whom recruit followers among humans. After death the spirits of their human followers join the good God in heaven, or go with the bad God to hell.

During most of the Biblical age, Jews had found justification and purpose for their lives in improving this world, and in their commitment to solidarity with the Jewish people. Greek thought, seeping into their imagination toward the close of the Biblical period, stimulated the development of individualism. As the central focus of personal concern shifted away from the community, to a clinging to the importance of one's own personality, there arose an anxiety about personal destiny. Then ideas about individual resurrection — life after death, reward or punishment — became popular.

By the first century these were the dominant ideas of the (Rabbis/Sages) Pharisees. The more traditional priest-oriented groups did not accept the teaching of personal reward or punishment after death. Jesus Josephson, who basically was a follower of the Pharisees, believed in the concept of heaven and hell. Because of his beliefs, and the fact that the New Testament was written during the period when this concept was dominant among the Rabbis, there is a great deal more stress placed on heaven and hell in the New Testament than in the Hebrew Bible. Thus, beliefs and anxieties about heaven and hell have a prominent place in the Christian imagination even today, whereas they scarcely prickle the surface of modern Jewish awareness.

When the Rabbis and the sages who followed the Pharisees looked for names for the realms of reward and punishment, of course, they wanted to use names from the Bible to legitimatize their ideas. For heaven or paradise they used the term Gan Eden, naming it after the mythical Garden in chapters II and III of Genesis. The name they selected for hell was taken from a valley, not far from the City of Jerusalem, which is mentioned several times in the Bible. It is called Gay Hinnom (the Valley of Hinnom), although at times it is referred to as Gay ben Hinnom (The Valley of the Son of Hinnom). This valley was used as a garbage dump. Frequently, fires burned there for days on end. More significantly, it was also used by the non-Jewish Caananites as a place where they sacrificed a first born child to their god Molech (Jeremiah 9:31-2 or 19:1-5).

According to the Book of Kings, when King Josiah attempted to reform Jewish society, he destroyed and defiled this place in an attempt to end the fiery sacrifice of children practiced there (2 Kings 23:10). In light of the vividness and horror of this derivation, it is not surprising to find the term Gehinnom became the most popular term for the realm of punishment used in Rabbinic literature, including the Kabbalah..

Speculations about Gehinnom, like those about Gan Eden, were always regarded as no more than speculations. The sages never accorded them the honor or emphasis reserved for discussion of our obligations toward our fellow humans. Speculations about heaven and hell were not related to performing the Mitsvot, they were merely exercises of the imagination. However, many of these concepts are interesting. And, as long as one isn't disturbed by their variety and frequent contradictions, one can find insights in the dicta of the sages, and in passages in the Zohar concerning heaven and hell.

The Zohar Hadash speaks of Gehenna (a westernized spelling of Gehinnom) as being divided into seventy-two compartments. Moses de Leon, the editor and part author of the Zohar, in a book under his own name, speaks of Gehenna as being divided into seven compartments in the upper Gehenna, and seven compartments in the lower Gehenna. However, the most important question about Gehenna is not the size or structure of Gehenna, but who goes there. The answer is surprising.

According to some Rabbis, everybody goes to hell. But while everybody goes, hardly anyone stays in hell, at least not forever.

Let us look at some of these ideas in detail, and see what we can learn from them.

The Zohar and other Kabbalistic sources theorize that even the righteous go to Gehenna. The righteous and the wicked differ in the purpose of their going, and the length of their stay. There is a lot to be said for the Zohar's conclusions. After all, no one is perfectly righteous. Even the best among us have shared with the worst among us at one time or another some common act, or error, or omision. Further, an essential part of being good is the desire to help those who are less well off. It is only natural, therefore, that the righteous would want to enter Gehenna to attempt to rescue those who are there. The righteous do not stay long in Gehenna, however. When they leave, they take with them some of those whom they have redeemed by their influence, or their example.

It is interesting to note that such popularizers of the torments of Christian hell as Dante, Milton, and contemporary revivalists, for all their imagination, have not added significantly to the horrors of the punishments of Gehenna's inmates listed in the Zohar. Tortured by thirst, they are burned by fire, scalding water, brimstone, heaping coals, boiling semen, fiery stones, and molten lead. Worms crawl up and down their bodies. Their flesh in pounded by hail, chewed by dogs and lions, stung by scorpions and snakes. And they are starved throughout this torment until finally in despair and frenzy, they eat their own flesh.

These descriptions sound so Christian that most Jews are astonished to discover that they come from medieval Jewish literature. The concepts of an after-life taught in Christianity and Islam were based on Pharisaic teachings. They were expanded and extended by Christians and Moslems, and then influenced medieval Jews in return.

If the Pharisaic and medieval Rabbis went for the idea of hell, condemning in their imagination those who died to a stay there, they were almost to a man successful in resisting the concept of eternal damnation. Gehenna actually resembles more the Catholic notion of purgatory than the Christian concept of hell. Most of the Rabbis who speculated about Gehenna agreed that the average person spends no more than twelve months there.

There were exceptions. A Talmudic statement indicated that some are punished for thirty days, some for sixty days, some for ninety days, and some stay in Gehenna for as long as six months. Rabbi Yohanan ben Nuri felt that the general period of punishment is only seven weeks. Another opinion quoted in the Talmud states that some sinners are punished no more than an hour. The Zohar also mentions an individual who was punished only for an hour and a half.

One interesting view in the Zohar indicates that a sinner's punishment lasts only as long as it takes the body to deteriorate. The passage says, "All sinners as long as their bodies are in the grave intact, are judged body and soul together, each in their own way. But as soon as the body is decayed, the punishment of the soul ceases". This interpretation reflects the Jewish view that the body should return to the earth and decay as quickly as possible. Judaism teaches that of all approaches to interring the dead, the best is a simple funeral using a plain wooden casket, which does not impede the natural processes of the body's decay. It would be ironic if those people who had wasted hundreds, even thousands of dollars on caskets made out of metal, and followed elaborate chemical procedures to preserve the body, were merely prolonging the sufferings of the dead.

The feeling that the time spent in Gehenna could be shortened by good deeds on earth is reflected in this Hassidic story:

A certain man who had fallen on bad times came to the Hassidic Rabbi of Apta for advice and intercession to help him obtain a dowry for his daughter. The Rabbi asked him how much money he had. He said, "One rouble, but I need a thousand."

The Rabbi reassured him that everything would be all right: "Godspeed and take the first business that comes along and the Lord will prosper you."

The man was puzzled but trusted his Rabbi and went on his way. He came to an inn and saw some diamond merchants discussing their wares. He walked up to their table and started studying the stones on the table.

One of the merchants noticed him and asked, "Would you like to buy a diamond?"

"Yes."

"How much money do you have in your purse?"

"One rouble."

The merchants burst out laughing and the one who owned the diamonds turned to him, saying, "Listen here. I've got a good deal for you, for the price of a rouble. Buy my Hereafter."

"All right, but on condition that you sign and seal the agreement in writing."

The merchant agreed and to the laughter of the company took out his pen and signed and sealed the agreement, handing the deed to the man. He then claimed his rouble, and turned back to his friends, making a big joke of the poor ahnook who had given away his last coin for a mirage.

The poor man, with a completely empty purse, had nothing to do, but open a volume of the Talmud, and retire to a corner to study. While he was reading, the wife of the diamond merchant entered. Now she was the true owner of the diamonds since all her husband's wealth had been brought in by her. Seeing the laughter, she asked her husband what the huge joke was. But, instead of joining in, when they told her the tale, she was profoundly shocked and told her husband: "Now that you have sold your Hereafter, you are as godless as a heathen. Come with me to the Rabbi and give me a divorce."

The merchant began to stammer and make excuses, saying that the transaction was only a joke, but he could not convince her.

"I shall not live with an outright heathen who has no share in the Hereafter."

The merchant sent a messenger to call the man over to his table. He said to the man, "Tell my wife it was all a joke. Here's your rouble; Hand me back that piece of paper."

But the man refused. "Business is business."

"All right," said the merchant. "I'll let you make a little profit."

"Little? I want nothing less than a thousand roubles."

"What! For that piece of paper?"

The woman interrupted: "Even if he demands five thousand roubles, you must redeem your Hereafter."

The merchant tried to bargain, offering him a hundred roubles, but the poor man explained that the Rabbi of Apta had advised him to clinch the first business deal that came his way with his last rouble in order to obtain the thousand roubles he needed for his daughter's dowry. "I shall not let you have the deed for even one kopeck less than the thousand."

The merchant finally had to part with the thousand roubles in order to buy back his Hereafter.

The woman then asked the poor man to do her the favour of obtaining an audience for her with the Rabbi of Apta.

"Certainly," he said.

At the audience, the woman asked the Rabbi: "While I am happy to have been able to do a poor man a good turn and help him marry off his daughter, I should like to know whether my husband's Hereafter is really worth the thousand roubles.

The Rabbi answered: "When he made the first deal, selling his Hereafter for one rouble, it wasn't worth even that. But when he struck the second bargain, helping another Jew to see his daughter safely married, his Hereafter became worth much more than a thousand roubles."

Behind the Rabbi's words was the belief that whatever the length of time the souls of the dead were punished in Gehenna, when their internment was over, they were entitled to enter Gan Eden where they would receive the rewards for the mitzvot they performed in life. This is expressed in the Talmudic statement, "All Israel have a place in the Hereafter."

In the nineteenth and twentieth centuries, Jews have returned to the attitudes of Biblical times. Few Jews today believe in a personal judgement after death. Most Jews think there is some existence after death but avoid defining it. The torments of Gehenna as literal predictions of the fate of the living, are rejected by all contemporary Jewish thinkers, who tend to interpret them symbolically; maintaining that the real consequence of evil is death: The righteous survive death, but sinners do not. Thus while anxieties about heaven and hell torture the Christian imagination even today, they scarcely prickle the composure of modern Jewish awareness.

The Zohar Hadash comments that the inmates of Gehenna never are called by name. We use the same practice in our prisons. Prisoners are depersonalized by being referred to by number rather than by name, a practice that makes good punishment but poor rehabilitation. People's behavior tends to reflect the way they are treated. Depersonalizing can only result in their behaving less humanely when they enter society, than they had before they were imprisoned.

The description in the Zohar to Exodus of inmates of Gehenna tied hand and foot with stone chains around their necks reminds me of a vision of heaven and hell which was given to a certain man. He saw the sinners seated around a sumptuous banquet table which had been heaped with delicious food and drink. But the men and women were chained, hand to hand, so that each time they tried to grab some food or drink, they were unable to reach the refreshments because the persons chained to their right and left also were stretching and pulling against the chains in order to grab something for themselves. The vision showed that the sinners' hunger and thirst grew worse hour upon hour, and day after day. Yet, although the food was so near that they could see the details of its texture, and smell its fragrance, never were they able to satisfy their need by so much as a taste.

Then the vision shifted to Gan Eden. Imagine the man's horror when he saw that here too, people were chained hand to hand around a sumptuous banquet table heaped with savory food and drink. Can it be, he wondered, that heaven is no better than hell? He looked again and saw that, indeed, it was Gan Eden, for although the people at this table were in chains, they were not hungry, neither did they thirst. In Gan Eden when a woman wants to eat, she speaks to her neighbor and the two of them reach out together to pick up the desired food. Hand chained to hand, they place the food in the mouth of she who desires food. If a man needs to drink, he speaks to his neighbor. The two cooperate, moving with care and grace, to bring drink to the one who is thirsty.

Still beholding the vision, the man realized its meaning: The true difference between Gan Eden and Gehenna does not consist of the physical environment, but in the difference in the nature of their inhabitants. Righteous people share and cooperate. They help each other and satisfy one another's needs. Evil people are selfish, indifferent to the needs of others, and grasping. They make their own Gehenna.

כָּל יִשְׂרָאֵל יֵשׁ לָהֶן חֵלֶק לָעוֹלָם הַבָּא.

Everyone has a place in the world to come.

REINCARNATION

Although people frequently ask what happens after death, they rarely wonder what happens before birth. Yet is it not just as easy, or as hard, to believe in life preceding birth, as to believe in life after death? Jewish mystics have a word for reincarnation. The Hebrew word גלגול *gilgul* means a cycle or a recycle. Thus the word can be used to indicate a concept of life prior to, and subsequent to, the life we now know.

You will not find this concept expressed anywhere in the Hebrew Bible, nor is it to be found in the Talmud. While the major Jewish philosophers have either ignored the possibility of reincarnation or actively rejected it, the mystic tradition, the Kabbalah, accepts גלגול *gilgul* as a fact of reality. The Kabbalists dispute only about the circumstances by which *gilgul* operates.

For years, perhaps even centuries, *gilgul* was a secret teaching, handed down from sage to disciple. But by the twelfth century, the teaching found its way into writing, in the *Sefer Ha'Behir,* which contains several parables and explanations based on the idea of *gilgul.* In this early text, גלגול *gilgul* applies only to human beings and not to animals. The author of the *Sefer Ha'Behir* did not believe that a human soul could be reincarnated into the body of an animal.

Most early Kabbalists in southern France and Spain, including Moses de Leon, the editor/author of the Zohar, did not regard גלגול *gilgul* as a universal law governing all creatures, like the Hindu concept of karma. In fact, these early Kabbalists did not conceive of *gilgul* as applying to all humans. *Gilgul* went into operation, they believed, after a soul had transgressed God's laws so seriously that it was necessary for the soul to go through another life in order to repent or atone for its previous transgressions. The common opinion in the Spanish Kabbalah is that the soul of a sinner would transmigrate three or four times after leaving the body in which the major sinning had been accomplished. But not many people sin so terribly that גלגול *gilgul* is necessary to redeem their souls.

As it spread, the concept of *gilgul* quickened the imaginations of those who encountered it. Of course, the time may have been particularly ripe for such a concept, for despite its original connotation of punishment, the essence of גלגול *gilgul* after all is the promise of another life. The "I" which does not really conceive of ceasing to be, interprets that promise as more life, an extension of the life it knows. Whether they believe or not, few people are repelled by the notion of reincarnation. In the following generations, the teaching of גלגול *gilgul* was expanded to promise future life for sinner and non-sinner alike. During this process, the idea that *gilgul* could result in the soul's being reborn into the body of an animal or even a plant was occasionally taught.

The first mention of the possibility of transmigrating into plant or animal forms came in the *Sefer Ha'Temunah*. By the fifteenth and sixteenth centuries, Kabbalists, especially those centered around Safed in the land of Israel, extended the principle of *gilgul* considerably. According to Rabbi Joseph Ashkenazi, everything in the world is in a constant state of flux, changing from one form to another. The Kabbalists of Safed accepted the point of view that souls could and did transmigrate into all forms of nature and through their teaching in the next century or two, it became a widespread, popular belief, especially among the Hassidim.

In addition to *gilgul*, there is the concept, somewhat related, of עיבור *ibbur*. Literally, עיבור *ibbur* means impregnation. This concept presents the idea that the soul enters another body at some point, often many years, after the body's conception. Implicit in the notion of עיבור *ibbur* is the belief that the soul is not "wearing" or assuming a new form, but invading the body of another personality, a body belonging to a different soul. *Ibbur* may occur when the soul of an especially righteous man is linked to the consciousness of another person for the purpose of doing a great mitzvah, or to be present at some special occasion as a reward for good deeds in a previous life. In this case the linkage would be limited and would be broken off without effort from the host.

More often, however, especially as the concept developed, עיבור *ibbur* was a hostile act of a wicked soul which was inflicted upon a wicked person's consciousness as punishment to both. In this instance, *ibbur* is a form of possession in which the invading soul clings stubbornly to its new body despite frantic efforts to expel it. Here we have the origin of the דיבוק *dybbuk,* a departed soul which invades the consciousness of a human for malevolent purposes.

Stories about דיבוקים *dybbukim* or demon possession were common throughout the ancient Middle East and the Roman Empire. There are none in the Hebrew Bible, but a few are scattered throughout the accounts in the New Testament which relate how Jesus Josephson obtained many of his followers by his success in casting out *dybbukim*. (Luke 8:22 & 33, 9:39-50; Mark 9:16-29; Matthew 15:28).

In the sixteenth and seventeenth centuries, rumors and charges of spirit possession became part of village life in Europe, and have come down to us in vivid detail in written and oral folk history. The spread of the concept of *gilgul* may have contributed to this reemergence of fears about spirit possession, but some more general influence must also have been at work.

It is quite likely that Jewish communities had been infected with the morbid fascination for witchcraft and satanism prevalent among the Christians throughout the Middle Ages. At the beginning of that period, the Church's witch hunts were essentially an attempt to root out heretics and the adherents of the ancient non-Christian religions of Europe. But after centuries of persecution a few of the old cults degenerated into satanism, their members in a mood of savage despair dabbling in occultism especially the arts of summoning evil spirits, and magic. In most cases, mentally ill people learned from the Church the bizarre behavior they weve supposed to do in order to contact the devil.

Although authentic satanist covens were non-existent, the frequent church led witch hunts had an effect on the popular imagination throughout Europe which was catastrophic. Many of the young and adventurous from all levels of society, villager to courtier, flirted with witchcraft. That in itself increased the growing fear and horror of satanism.

Communication and travel being difficult, in those days popular movements and fads moved slowly and irregularly. It was as though a plague of demons had struck Europe, striking village after village, city after city, kingdom after kingdom. At times the epidemic died down only to pop up again a few miles or a few decades away. Many people, male and female, of all ages, complained of, or evidence, the symptoms of spirit possession. Others were the innocent victims of fearful and hostile accusations of spirit possession.

Medical examination of our contemporaries who feel they are possessed by evil spirits reveals that in actuality most of them suffer from certain forms of schizophrenia, characterized by hallucinations and panic, or from multiple personality. A person with multiple personality is likely to interpret the "surfacing" of the repressed personality as possession by a *dybbuk*. This is especially the case when the dominant personality conforms to the community's standards of behavior while the repressed personality, struggling with intermittent success to gain control of the individual's consciousness, desires and acts out socially unacceptable behavior. Indeed this is a kind of possession, the invasion of one aspect of an individual's personality by another. But in these cases only one soul is involved, the soul of a sick and tormented individual and not of a *dybbuk*.

The religious leaders among the Christians were overwhelmed by calls on their services as exorcists. Even the Jews were influenced by the contemporary currents. A new type of ex official "professional" emerged whose major function was to save the God fearing from the invasion of a *dybbuk*.

Among the Jewish communities of Eastern Europe in the sixteenth and seventeenth centuries, such a person was called a *ba'al shem*. The founder of the Hassidic movement began his career (like Jesus Josephson seventeen centuries before him) as an exorciser of demons. Today psychoanalysts perform a similar function. Recent studies by the National Institute of Mental Health have shown that psychotherapists have a success rate that is just as high as that of American Indian medicine men. Although the theories and the terminology are different, the psychodynamics are not so unlike.

Dybbukim, however, are only a small although rather sensational part of the general principle of *gilgul*, and *gilgul* is only one of several possible theories of what follows death. Judaism takes no dogmatic stand about the question of life after death. The Bible, which is the most authoritative text in the Jewish tradition, indicates in a few places that there is some kind of existence after death, but does not describe the nature of that existence. Nor does the Bible teach that there is a heaven or hell, a final judgement, or a process of reincarnation. The Rabbis of the Talmudic period did teach that after death there was reward and punishment, a heaven and a place of short-term punishment which could more properly be called purgatory. But the Talmud does not teach that there is a cycle of *gilgul*.

The Kabbalah and its most authoritative text, the Zohar, does teach the existence of a cycle of reincarnation. Some Kabbalists see the cycle as limited to specific individuals, usually for reasons of transgression. Other Kabbalists, especially in the later development of this concept, viewed reincarnation as a general process through which all souls go, to be followed ultimately by a reward or punishment in an existence not on this earth.

Modern Jews, as inheritors of these varying traditions, can be found to believe any, or all, of these ideas, as well as to believe with the author of the Book of Ecclesiastics that there is nothing after death. The author of that Biblical book of disbelief teaches that "the dead know not anything, neither have they any more reward. Even the memory of them is forgotten." (Ecclesiastes 9:5) He also comments, "That which befalls the sons of man befalls the animals. The same thing befalls them both. As one dies so dies the other. Yea, they all have one breath. So that man has no preeminence above beast. It is all vanity. All go to one place. All are of the dust and all return to the dust." (Ecclesiastes 3:19-21).

Thus we are free to speculate freely. And the resurgence of interest in reincarnation which has spread throughout the western world in the last few years, makes it worthwhile to take another, closer look at *gilgul*.

I myself, did not believe in the concept of גלגול *gilgul*, until very recently.

Then, in my studies of Kabbalah, I came across a fourteenth century text, Sefer Ha'pliya, the Book of Marvels, which speaks of a special form of *gilgul* which can actually be seen in operation. This is the *gilgul* following the occasion of a Jewish soul being "cut off or lost" from the Jewish people.

The means of separation do not seem to be important. It could have been volitional, accidental, or under duress. It could have been the result of a sin or of a mitzvah. A Jewish infant, orphaned because its parents had been killed saving the lives of others, and raised as a gentile, or a person who had deliberately turned his back on his own people and converted to a non-Jewish religion. Whatever the reason for the original separation, three, four, or more generations later, the displaced soul is reborn into his family line. The soul is reborn as its own descendant and consequently as an infant in a gentile family. Born a gentile, the infant is, naturally, raised and educated as a gentile. But the yearning of the soul to return to its own people is so great that eventually it finds its way back to the Jewish religion, people, and culture.

Of course, not all non-Jews who convert to Judaism are the reincarnated souls of Jews who had been separated from Judaism in former lives. There is, however, one characteristic which hints at the indentification of those who are; a single Jewish ancestor in their gentile family tree. And there is a familiar outline to their path to Judaism.

The religious tradition of their birth never seems to fit them well. They cannot completely accept it. Their doubts grow. They begin searching here and there, restlessly. Finally, they are drawn to a particular Jew, or a group of Jews, and by this means gradually become part of the Jewish people. Much to their surprise, frequently such people discover after they have converted to Judaism that one of their great grandparents had been a Jew.

Since I learned of this concept from the Sefer Ha'pliya, I have come across at least a dozen instances of its workings. There is not enough space in this book to describe them all, but I will outline four such histories as examples of *gilgul* according to the Sefer Ha'pliya.

I met a young man who could not accept the Lutheran religion and training he had known all his life. For years his mind had churned with doubt. He had studied a number of different religious movements and substitutes for religion. Nothing seemed to satisfy him or calm his inner turbulence. Eventually he chanced to meet some young Jewish men and women, and quickly they became fast friends. He joined them in a trip to Israel, and he liked what he found there so much that he stayed for ten months. One night, standing in front of the Western wall, it came to him with a feeling of inner certainty that he needed to identify himself with the Jewish people. He returned to the United States and studied with a Rabbi. Finally, he converted formally to Judaism. It was only natural that his family had been distressed by this sequence of events,and had opposed his conversion step by step until the deed was done. Then his mother broke down and told him what she had been keeping secret, fearful that it would add more weight to his religious yearnings: his great, great grandfather had been Jewish.

Another example comes from the midwest. There, one day a teenage girl climbed up to the family attic in search of a costume to wear to a masquerade. Rummaging in one of the trunks, she happened to open an old cloth bag. It contained two little boxes with long black straps attached to them. Curious, she took them to her parents, asking what they were. They knew nothing except that they were heirlooms, handed down from parent to child in their family for three or four generations. More and more curious, she went around town with the boxes, hoping to find someone who could indentify them.

Finally, the curator of the local museum recognized them as tifillin, the special ritual objects used by orthodox Jews in their morning prayers, when the straps are wrapped around the forehead and right arm. With that clue, the teenager began delving into the family history in earnest and learned that these particular tifillin had belonged to her great grandfather who had immigrated from Germany in the 1850's. Shortly after he and wife arrived and settled down, the wife had died, leaving him not only a widower but a widower among gentiles in a strange land.

Eventually, he found a new wife. Their children followed the religious traditions of their gentile mother. They, too in time, married non-Jews and by the third generation even the memory of their Jewish heritage had been forgotten. Fascinated by this story, the young woman began studying the culture and traditions of her great grandfather's people. In college, she sought out Jewish students to learn more about Judaism. She did not rest, perhaps she could not rest, until she too, was part of the Jewish people.

I came across several other examples of *gilgul* in the newspapers. An Israeli newspaper reported that in 1965 a young girl arrived in Israel and asked the Tel Aviv rabbinate to be converted to Judaism. She was the great granddaughter of the well-known German poet, Heinrich Heine.

"The rabbinate refused to give the name of the girl, who is 21 and lives with her parents in West Germany. She told the rabbis that she has wanted to become Jewish since she was 16 when she saw a film about the Nazi slaughter of European Jewry. She said that she then learned that her famous great grandfather who was born in 1797, was Jewish. The secretary of the Tel Aviv Rabbinical Court said that the girl gave an impression of 'a serious personality' and that he had recommended prompt consideration of her request."

Another newspaper reported that a 36-year-old Baptist Pastor from London and his 24-year-old Welsh-born wife, were converted to orthodox Judaism after completing the necessary steps including study, circumcision and immersion in the Mikvah (a ritual bath). Pastor Francis McHaddington took the Jewish name, Samuel Golding. The Golding family name comes from his maternal grandmother who was born Jewish. Her grandfather was Reb Golding, a Chassidic rabbi.

The increase in conversion to Judaism is part of the messianic upheaval and the return of "cut off or lost" Jewish souls is part of the ingathering of the exiles. I could give additional examples, but the reader will already understand that the chances of these "returns" occurring randomly are very high. There are over 200 million gentiles in the United States and only 5 to 10 thousand of them become Jewish each year. That many of these people are descendants from "lost Jews", is truly amazing.

In addition to the highly specific evidence from converts to Judaism, the laws of physics seem to provide much more general support for the basic idea of *gilgul*. Modern science teaches the "law" of the conservation of matter and energy. This is not the kind of law legislated, but an expression of what scientists have observed and believe to be unvaryingly true of the universe. Nothing in the universe ever really is destroyed. It is only transformed. Matter changes form and shape, but the atoms composing matter are much more stable. At the most they can be subject to fission or fusion. When combined or divided they form new elements and release or absorb energy. Even this is atomic transformation rather than atomic destruction for the subatomic particles recombine into matter and energy. Matter and energy only change form, they are not "used up."

In the world, we see life forms continually come into being, develop, multiply, age, and die. Objects come into being and are destroyed.

Underneath both these processes is a grouping and regrouping of molecular structure. Molecules form and break apart. From their "parts" — the atoms which make them up — new molecules come into being. Molecules like the objects in our visible world are transient. Each atom in its now ancient existence has been part of many molecules, but its own form remains the same unless it is part of a nuclear reaction. Most atoms are hundreds of millions of years old, and have undergone thousands, even millions of molecular transformations.

When a person dies and is buried in the ground, his body begins to decay. This means that the flesh and organs of his body and the molecules which make up those structures undergo changes. One could say that these molecules also are "dying": they cease to exist as those particular molecules which they were in the body structure. They often have broken down into their component atoms. The atoms themselves, however, do not break down. Their structure is unaltered.

The atoms which had been the person's body recombine with other atoms to form different molecules and enter the ground in which the body had been buried. There, as part of the soil, they remain for months or centuries or millenia depending on what chances to happen. They may remain in the soil and become part of a mountain. Or they may enter the food chain by being absorbed through the roots into the sap of a plant to be carried to and become part of its stalk or leaves. Later still, that plant might be eaten by an animal. Then these same atoms may become part of the animal's body. If that animal is eaten by a person, those atoms again may become part of another human being.

Before they become part of us, the atoms in our bodies already had long histories of existence. Most of the atoms in our bodies have existed from the beginning of the universe. They were formed in the first 30 minutes of creation. These atoms floated in space for eons. Some of them were part of immense gas clouds. They condensed into stars which burned for a few billion years fusing them into new elements and finally ended in gigantic explosions called supernova (producing as much energy in a day as the sun does in a hundred thousand years). Most of the mass of a supernova is ejected into space and later becomes part of new gas clouds that condense to form stars and planets.

All of our body's atoms have been on earth for the last four to five billion years. In the last billion years most of the atoms in our bodies have participated in the evolutionary sequence of life on earth. Some of your atoms floated on the ocean as part of an algae colony, perhaps later some of them were part of a trilobite living on the sea floor, later still, fixed in the plant life then extending over this once bare earth. The stuff of our bodies may have muscled a dinosaur's body or winged a pterydactyl. Some of our atoms could have been in the brain of an australopithecus − the protohuman race whose bones were discovered in Africa by Mary and Louis Leaky. Some may have been part of a Mongol khan, a Babylonian queen, an Aztec noble, a Spanish conquistador, a Watusi dancer, an Eskimo hunter, a Boston sea captain, or a felon hanged and quartered in the London of Queen Elizabeth I for stealing the silver buckles from a rich lord's shoes.

If survival through many lives, many forms of existence is true for our bodies, as scientists assure us it is, why may it not also be true of the spiritual elements of our being? Just as we each have a body, so each of us has a separate personality. The body is composed of molecules which in turn are made up of atoms. The personality is composed of electrical impulses in the brain. Or course, the body is more than a random pile of atoms, and the personality is more than a simple series of electrical impulses. In both cases the patterning is critical.

As the infant grows and experiences, the patterning of electrical impulses within the brain alters in a unique way that is the personality of David, or Liz, or fat little Eddie just learning how to work a spoon. The process of modification begins before birth and continues until the brain dies. Personality continually is being shaped by experience; although memory and habit are counter influences to change, and certain aspects of personality seem to be predisposed by genetic structure.

Few people doubt the reality of the physical environment "out there" − a complex, patterning of atoms. Few people believe that their own bodies are less real, or that they do not actually interact with the physical environment − a "star system" of atoms moving through the great "universe" of atoms which constitute our little planet. (The micro worlds of molecules, atoms, and their subatomic particles do possess design similarities to the macro worlds of star systems, galaxies, and the universe itself.)

But the process of our perception of the world about us, including our perception of our own bodies, once the initial mechanical or chemical contact with the physical environment "out there" has been made, is nothing more and nothing less than a flow of electrical impulses in the nervous system and the brain. The light wave or sound wave impinges upon our retina or inner ear, the alien chemical contacts sensory cells in our mouth and nose, or an object presses against nerve endings in our skin and muscle. But, subsequently − the next step in the process − these physical events are encoded into patterns of electrical impulses. Our awareness of these events depends completely on the brain's ability to decode the patterns of electrical impulses which it receives from the sites of contact. Without the process of encoding and decoding, without the transmission of electrical impulses, there would be no sensation. Similarly, our memory, our emotions, and thought itself are imputs of a nonphysical type depending on the flow of electrical energy. That energy flow, these impulses, the mind, the personality, what happens to them when the body dies and decays?

Just as there is a "law" of the conservation of matter, so also physicists tell us, energy is neither created or destroyed in an ultimate sense, within our universe. Energy flows back and forth from one of its states to another, from one kind of energy into matter and back again. Burn a tree and you have heat and carbon. Put a kettle of water on the log fire and some of that heat converts the fluid water to gas (water vapor). And some of that steam pushes the kettle's top up into the air: the energy of combustion transforming first into mechanical energy then into potential energy. Similarly, sound energy can set off a dance of kinetic energy resulting in heat. Enough heat can transform iron and an alloy into steel. It's an endless show, this shifting of one form of energy into matter, of one form of matter into another form — back and forth in a cosmic kaleidescope of patterns which has been going on since the beginning of the universe.

The energy forces of the personality must undergo a transformation no less radical than the transformation which the body undergoes following death. Philosophers long have disputed whether the components of energy are transformed in the same way that the components of the body are, so that, although there is a survival energy in the ultimate sense after death, it is not survival of the particular energy patterns which makes up the individual personality. Some philosophers speculate that after the body's death, the energy patterns which had made up the personality break up into separate components and become part of the Great World Soul (frequently the process is called returning to God, or merging with God) or the components reform with other components to form a "new soul" attached to a new body and are born, develop, and ultimately die to repeat the process once again.

If this latter concept is true, energy reincarnates, but not the unique personality. And with no survival of the unique personality, there is no possibility of the memory of past lives surviving. The old pattern would be gone, utterly; just as completely gone as is the supernova from which came the carbon atoms of our bodies. That star is no more as it was, but its atoms "live" in perhaps a million other forms, living and inanimate. In this view of reincarnation, the old personality is gone, but its energy "lives on" in differrent forms. Clearly, this is the least attractive of the concepts of reincarnation because it is our personalities that we know, love, and wish to retain.

Nevertheless, this line of reasoning does establish a baseline for the concept of גלגול *gilgul*. Death is not complete destruction or a meaningless void. Death is at least a recycling and recreation of the materials of the universe. Even at this baseline, death is part of life, part of the continual pattern of birth, growth, decay, destruction, and rebirth. This baseline gives us the assurance that our minds and personalities are as much a part of the universe as they are part of ourselves. They do not simply come to an end. They reach a new stage, a new type of development.

Whether more of the individual survives than a handful of atoms and a flow of energy remains unproved. But the evidence from converts to Judaism with Jewish ancestors, would seem to indicate that at least for some, perhaps for all, death is only a transition.

כָּל־הַנְּחָלִים הֹלְכִים אֶל־הַיָּם וְהַיָּם אֵינֶנּוּ
מָלֵא, אֶל־מְקוֹם שֶׁהַנְּחָלִים הֹלְכִים שָׁם הֵם
שָׁבִים לָלָכֶת.

All the streams flow into the sea but the sea is not filled. They return to a place where the streams flow again.

THE MYSTERY OF ISRAEL'S SURVIVAL

Two of the most important subjects in Kabbalistic speculation are the reasons behind Jewish martyrdom and the miracle of Jewish survival. These areas are almost always avoided in English treatments of Kabbalah. The Jewish people is the oldest nation in the western world. Over three thousand years ago, when King David ruled in Jerusalem, there were dozens of other peoples and civilizations throughout the Middle East, North Africa, and Europe. None has survived to the present. The ancient Egyptians, the Cretans, the Babylonians, the Sumerians, the Akkadians, the Greeks, the Romans, the Persians: they and their empires have disappeared.

Of course, people continue to live in those countries; and many of them, perhaps most of them, are biological descendants of the citizens of those ancient nations, but the contemporary peoples do not speak the same language as their ancestors, or have the same religion, or maintain a continuous culture or tradition linking them with the ancient culture of their land. Their laws have been completely transformed, their holidays are different, their culture is new. A modern Egyptian speaks Arabic not Egyptian; is a Moslem, not a believer in Isis; and reads the Koran and not the Pyramid Texts or the prophet Ipu-wer.

Of all the nations in existence in the western world in the days of King David, only the Jewish people today still has the same language, the same religion, the same national holidays, the same tradition, and the same historical continuity. Much has been changed in the course of those three thousand years. A great deal has been added; a lot has been subtracted. Changes and innovations have been constant. Yet, just as an adult is a product of a teenager, and the teenager is the product of the child, and the child is a product of a baby, so the present Jewish people are the product of those people who originated four thousand years ago in the days of Abraham, Isaac, and Jacob, who followed Moses, and after his death entered the land of Israel under the leadership of Joshua, established a capital in Jerusalem under David, and built the Temple of the Lord under Solomon.

In the entire world there are only two other peoples of similar antiquity;

the Hindus and the Chinese. Why have these three and only these three peoples survived?

It is not difficult to explain the survival of the Chinese. Part of their survival lies in the accident of geography. The Chinese lived far away from most other civilizations and cultures at the extreme eastern end of Asia. They were cut off from India by the Himalayas whose soaring peaks permitted only dedicated individuals such as Buddhist missionaries, diplomats, and the emissaries of wealthy merchants, to go back and forth.

The Chinese achieved unity fairly early in their culture. Shi-huang-Ti, who died in 210 BCE, bound the various warring states into one centrally-ruled empire. Although the empire broke up and was reunited several times, the ideal of unity always remained. Finally, and perhaps most importantly, even then the Chinese were very numerous, more numerous by far than the peoples with whom they came in contact, such as the Koreans, the Japanese, the Vietnamese, the Thais, and the Mongols who, despite their successful conquest of the Chinese, were ultimately absorbed by them. This numerical superiority helped insure their social survival, and therefore their cultural continuity.

The Hindus, on the other hand, were in contact with many other highly developed civilizations, and were influenced by Persians, Greeks, Arabs, and Mongols. They survived, partly because of their large population, but mostly because their religion was polytheistic and their culture was syncretistic. The alien influences that swept over them were added indiscriminately to what was already on hand. All the different ideas, foreign traditions, differing points of view, strange gods and goddesses were swallowed up and converted, not necessarily well-chewed or digested, into existing traditions.

Even new peoples were ingested and given a place in the Hindu caste system, which allowed the newcomers to keep their own customs, and made use of their skills and labor, but by isolating them socially, rendered their influence impotent. They became merely another undigested bit in the Hindu social body.

Jews however, have always had a small population, and have never been, isolated from other civilizations. They have always lived not merely adjacent to, but actually within, a larger civilization. From the time of Abraham, who left his Babylonian-Assyrian homeland and journeyed to the Land of Israel, Jews have almost always been a part of whatever civilization was currently the most advanced in the western world. They participated in almost every major culture in the western world. Usually contributing more to their host culture than they took from it. Their impact on their surroundings has been much greater than their limited numbers would lead one to believe.

Because they were aware of being a minority, Jews have felt a sense of uniqueness coupled with a sense of destiny dating back to the promises Abraham felt he had been given by the Lord of the Universe. The Jews survived for more than eighteen hundred years without a homeland. They lived for generations in various countries in Asia, Africa, Europe, and most recently, in the Americas. During all this time, they took part in the world around them, influencing and being influenced by it, but they never lost their identity as Jews. They were not assimilated into the greater numbers of the surrounding culture, and even more amazingly, they survived the frequent attempts to destroy them.

The Bible records the attempts of Pharoah and of Haman to destroy the Jewish people. During the Crusades many communities were wiped out by the Christians. At the time of the Bubonic Plague, superstitious peasants in Europe, believed the Jews had caused the sickness, by poisoning the wells in an alliance with the Devil, and massacred thousands of Jews. At various times, with much bloodshed and suffering, Jews have been exiled from England, France, Spain, Portugal, and Germany. They were massacred in Poland and Russia during the seventeenth century.

The Nazis attempted to destroy the Jewish people completely and, indeed, succeeded in killing almost six million of them, one-third of all the Jews in the entire world. Today, parts of the Arab world still refuse to try to work out a peace with Israel, vowing not to rest until they drive the Jews once more from their ancient homeland. The Russians still try to forcibly assimilate us, and the "only one way" Christians to convert us.

The survival of the Jewish people in the midst of all these adverse circumstances taxes the rational mind. Many people, both Jewish and not, feel that Jewish survival is a miracle, the clearest evidence of the existence of God, the Lord of history, who does from time to time intervene in the course of human events.

If this belief is true, and I believe that it is true, how are we to understand the extent and degree of Jewish suffering? If God intervened in human events to save the Jewish people from extermination, why didn't He intervene sooner to protect His Chosen Peoples' lives and comfort? The Kabbalah puts both the suffering of the Jewish people and their ultimate survival in a special metaphysical context.

Before we can grasp that context, we must understand the special nature of time as a divine dimension. Most religions are spatially oriented. They have a holy place, a spot within the church which is holy, or a holy being —

a person whose picture is portrayed, or whose image is fashioned in stone. The Jewish tradition perceives divinity through the dimension of time. Jews honor holy time — Sabbath and Holydays. Our God is not the spirit of Nature — the lord of the rain, the earth, or the sunset. The spiritual leaders of the Jewish people found their God in the history and destiny of the Jewish people.

To understand the difference, let's make some simple comparisons. Christians, Buddhists, and Moslems celebrate the birthday of their founders. Jews do not celebrate the birthday of anyone — not of Abraham or Moses or David. None of the Jewish Holydays refers to an event that occurred to, or was important for, an individual. They refer rather to events that happened to the Jews as a people. The redemption from slavery in Egypt is the occasion of the Passover seder. The successful revolution against the Syrian Greeks is the occasion for Hannukah. The giving of the Torah to the Jewish people at Sinai is celebrated on Shavu'ot. The creation of the state of Israel in 1947/48 is the occasion for the Jews' newest Holyday — Yom Atzmaoot, the day of Israel's independence.

The Jewish religion is the outgrowth of the experience of the Jewish people through events to which they ascribe transcendent meaning. Every people has a history, but many people pay no attention to their own history. It is meaningless to them. The Jewish people know that their history is more than a series of fortuitous events; it is the enactment on this earth of a divine plan. The history of the Jews has a goal; the Jews have a destiny. That destiny is not to have fun, be happy, or even live in peace, it is to fullfill our historic role.

Jews invented history as we know it today. Most cultures have been ahistorical; they did not think in historical terms. They merely noted events, but saw no connection between them. They did not perceive that history had a direction. The ancient Egyptians, for example, would write chronicles: "In the fifth year of King So, there was a war; in the seventh year, there was a famine." But the royal chroniclers made no attempt to link these events together, explaining their cause-and-effect relationships, noting the flow of events. The Egyptian, the Hindu, and the Greek philosophers considered truth universal, static, unchanging. Events were the stuff of poetry, of epic story-telling, but they were not the source of truth. They had no religious value. They indicated no purpose. Events are unique, not universal; they are relative, not absolute; they are subjective experiences, not objective science. Only the Jews found the truth of God in human history.

History was invented three times: by the Jews in the Tenth Century BCE

(Before the Common Era), the oldest historical work, being the Book of Samuel; by the Greeks in the Fifth Century BCE starting with the history of Herodotus; and in the Second Century BCE by the Chinese, with Ssu-ma T'en's great history of the rise of the Han Dynasty, The Shih Chi. India never did develop independently a concept of history because its sages were concerned with the eternal and the unchanging underneath all the superficial variety. Not until a very late date did the Hindus import the concept of history from the Moslems.

The Bible perceives time as the divine dimension. The future is the realm of the possible. It is free will which opens the future. The unpredictability of the future is the evidence that free will truly exits. In the beginning, before God created the universe, there was no disharmony or conflict in existence. There also was no change. Nor was there any choice. Even time did not exist, for time is the measure of change, and the future is the possibility of choice. God could have created a universe which was in perfect harmony, without conflict or evil. But in order to do so, the Divine will would have had to fill the universe. There would have been no room for any other will. There would have been no possibility of any other being with a free will. There would be no future, merely the determined existence of the perfect universe.

In order for there to be creatures capable of exercising free will and making moral choices it was necessary for the Infinite to be limited. This process is called in Kabbalah, צימצום tsimtsum. (see "Intelligent Life in Outer Space"). This contraction, or voluntary self limitation of the Master of the universe, is what permits all intelligent creatures on the various planets in our universe to exercise their free will to choose good or evil. Since many intelligent creatures do choose evil there is in our world conflict, disharmony, and violence.

For billions of years on our planet there was no war, no oppression, no injustice, no evil. Before the evolution of mankind there were no creatures capable of choosing either good or evil. The possibility of evil was brought into the world by mankind. The possibility of good was also brought into the world by mankind.

The ultimate goal of history, human history on this planet, and divine history in the universe, is תיקון Tikun, the restoration, the fixing-up of the disharmonious conflict-ridden societies on the planets in our universe. When the societies and civilizations of the intelligent beings throughout the universe have all reached the level where they freely choose the good, then the creatures' acts will be in harmony with the Divine Will. We will be Godlike because we will act so that our will and God's will are one.

This is the stage which humanity will reach after the transition of the Messianic Age (see "The Coming of the Messianic Age"). It is the destiny of mankind, and the particular destiny of the Jewish people, to bring about the תיקון *Tikun* on the planet Earth, which will restore our part of the Divine harmony which existed before the צימצום *tsimtsum*. When all the intelligent civilizations in the universe have reached this stage of *Tikun,* and are joined together in a universal harmony, the universe will be fulfilled. Jews suffer more than other people because our role is central to the battle between good and evil on this planet, and because the victim survives each evil only to be challenged by the next evil. Soon we shall triumph over the ultimate enemy and the supreme value of the struggle, and the suffering, will be evident to all.

וְאֶעֶשְׂךָ לְגוֹי גָּדוֹל, וַאֲבָרֶכְךָ וַאֲגַדְּלָה שְׁמֶךָ
וֶהְיֵה בְּרָכָה, וַאֲבָרְכָה מְבָרֲכֶיךָ וּמְקַלֶּלְךָ
אָאֹר, וְנִבְרְכוּ בְךָ כֹּל מִשְׁפְּחֹת הָאֲדָמָה.

I will make you into a great nation. I will bless you, and make you famous. You will be a blessing. I will bless those who bless you and those who curse you I will afflict. All the earth's families will be blessed through you.

THE COMING OF THE MESSIANIC AGE

Jews and Christians who use Biblical prophecies to predict the future, are saying that the first tremors of the Messianic Age are upon us. They point to many signs: The devastation of entire regions by natural and man-made causes. Unbridled violence. Terror.

Change—technical, economic, political, social—outpacing the human capacity to learn and adjust. A flood of peoples torn from their roots, pushed from country to country. The population explosion.

Oppression of individual rights increasing together with individual irresponsibility. The energy crisis. Cataclysmic weapons of war. The alarming destruction of our natural environment.

The massacre of six million Jews by the Nazis, followed by the fulfillment of the nineteen-hundred-year-old dream of the Jewish people to return to their homeland as citizens of an independent nation. ·

This isn't the first time in history that people have predicted the end of the world, or that the millennium was coming. But today anticipation of a new age is stirring scholastic minds as well as the emotions of enthusiasts. I myself believe that the beginning of the Messianic Age has already swept down upon us.

Humanity first heard about a new age to come in the 7th and 8th centuries, before the common era, when the Biblical prophets Jeremiah and Isaiah revealed God's promise to them, that He will someday establish a new society of harmony and justice for all people and all nations. According to the prophets, God himself referred to this new age as a time of redemption and, since the Lord promised He would send a Messiah to help mankind enter into the new society, it has also come to be known as the Messianic Age. Jeremiah and Isaiah were not the first prophets to speak of this vision. Others also raised their voices to describe Divine visions and promises of a Messianic Age. The conviction and urgency of their messages have survived time and translation. More arresting is the similarity of their main theme . . . and their differences in detail.

All the prophets agreed that the era of peace and justice was contingent on human repentance—an experience and expression of increased moral and spiritual consciousness. They all saw the Holy Land rebuilt in prosperity, and an independent Jewish State established in the land of Israel. They all foresaw an era of peace and justice, with a significant improvement in the quality of life.

They did not prophesy utopia, nor is the Messianic Age of their visions an ideal world existing somewhere else in space, or a time after our life on earth is at an end. Their visions make plausible an interpretation of God's promise as the next major turning point in civilization, not a reign of goodness imposed upon humanity by a *deus ex machina,* but an accomplishment humans, with God's halp, can achieve *if* they struggle hard enough at the right tasks. From this point of view, God was telling the prophets that an era of international peace, justice, and better living conditions will be achieved on a global scale.

Human creativity in the area of science has already improved the quality of human life by reducing our helplessness before the forces of nature. Flood control is becoming more sophisticated. Seismologists' accuracy in predicting earthquakes is increasing, and long term projects are underway to defuse earthquakes and volcanic eruptions. Eventually, rainmaking will put a damper on droughts, and even the possibility of taming hurricanes and tornados is being explored.

Medical science has already stopped the periodic thinning out of whole population groups by plague. Many of the killer and maiming diseases, the crippling consequences of accidents, and dangerous metabolic problems have been drastically reduced. In most parts of the world at least, women no longer bear their young in agony and fear of their lives.

Next on the list and coming up fast is control of genetic defects and the diseases of age. Doing away with death, on the other hand, seems not only impossible but undesirable. Without death, there would be no room for new generations and the fresh perspectives and possibilities they bring (see "The Secrets of Creation"). Nevertheless, it's obvious that in the next quarter century the human lifespan will be extended somewhat and its years of health, vigor, and physical beauty will be stretched out impressively.

The technical leap forward needed to further our control of nature is clearly within our grasp. Putting an end to the misery caused by social injustice seems both further away and less certain. Its achievement depends on enormous strides in spiritual and moral development. However, it's heartening to see already underway various movements toward spiritual growth.

Think of the one million children massacred by the Nazis during the Second World War. Think of the tens of thousands of children living in

Hiroshima and Nagasaki in 1945 when the atom bombs fell. Think of the children of Korea, Biafra, Viet Nam and Cambodia. They have suffered for no more reason than being in the wrong place at the wrong time. This kind of suffering results from poor judgment, wanton irresponsibility, and immorality in both governments and the governed. The governed may lack the intent of doing evil, but if they acquiesce to it, they must share in the responsibility. Group morality rests on private conscience.

Few people want children to suffer, but here is the pinch. To repent of responsibility for their suffering requires a tremendous effort by us as individuals in disciplining our emotions, in contributing time and materials, and in exercising cool, creative intelligence. Up to this point in civilization, most individuals have always boggled at making the necessary effort to create and sustain group morality.

Yet to successfully channel human aggressiveness away from exploitation for private gain into creative activity for the common good, requires group pressure and group planning. When we have achieved that, we will see senseless violence disappear and warfare whimper to an end. Another ancient dream will have come true; God's promise to the prophets will be fulfilled: There will be peace among nations and all people will work together in justice and harmony.

But God did not promise human beings were going to become perfect. Frustration and personal limitations will continue in the Messianic Age. Difference in talents, in personality, and in sensory and intellectual abilities will go on creating differences in opportunity and in point of view. Rivalry will not disappear, nor disappointment when two people want something only one of them can have. The anguish of rejection when love is not returned will not vanish. Nor will the misery of two people in love whose personalities or goals are incompatible, or the grief of loss caused by death or distance. Envy, irritation, anxiety, anger will flicker in and out of our personal relations.

These emotional responses are part of the human condition, like having arms instead of wings. They have their pluses and minuses, but we are better off with them than without them. We can cope with our private emotions and even grow from coping with them. We are not helpless victims of our personal relationships as we are of natural disasters and social injustice. As participants, we can shape personal relationships in terms of our values and goals. Or, if our partners refuse to give on issues threatening our vital commitments, we can terminate the relationship. With practice we can become skilled in adjusting to others' personalities and needs, in shaping relationships, in learning to accept loss, and in creating an atmosphere of joyful involvement around us. Ultimately, personal happiness is the result of one's values, decisions, courage, and persistently applied efforts.

No, the Messianic Age will not be a period of perfection. It will be better than perfect, offering us a peaceful, natural, and just political environment with wonderful challenges for personal growth, and the whole universe to explore.

Some people believe that it is possible to calculate the exact dates and events of the Messianic Age. They expect visions and prophecies recorded in the Bible Rabbinic literature to apply literally and precisely to the events of our own times, thousands of years after the predictions were made. This is fatalism; it would be possible only if God had foreordained human destiny.

We are not puppets being jerked about in roles assigned to us thousands of years ago. Human beings are free agents who must make their own choices and cope with the consequences of those choices. God did not predetermine destiny, not for humanity, not for a culture, not for an individual. We can use Biblical and Rabbinical prophecy as a guide to understand the significance of what is happening to us. We can use it as a guide to the kinds of behavior needed to hasten the Coming of the Messianic Age. We can draw from it the incentive to make the tremendous effort needed to direct our destiny, and the destiny of the human race towards the Messianic Age.

The visions themselves were only possibilities. The interaction between nations, and between God and humanity, can take many different directions. Not all the Messianic prophecies will be fulfilled. They cannot, as some call for events negated by other prophecies. Nor will fulfillment of prophecies always be exactly in the manner foreseen.

Mystical visions are projected by the personality and the cultural background of the seer. Imagery that would fit our time would have been unintelligible in the days of the prophets and the intervening centuries. Their followers would have renounced the visions; the prophecies would have been lost, depriving future generations of hope. It is better to communicate with future generations by using imagery of the present, than to use language the immediate audience cannot understand. As events occur, making it possible for the predictions to be realized, their meanings become clear. Only now that we are decades into the חבלי המשיח *Hevlay Hamoshe'ah,* the birthpangs of the Messiah, can we understand some of its most important features.

One of Zechariah's prophecies illustrates how a prophecy's

interpretation becomes easier as the event arrives: "Behold a day of the Lord 'cometh (the Messianic Age) when thy spoil shall be divided in the midst of thee. I will gather all nations against Jerusalem to battle, and the city shall be taken, the houses rifled, the women ravished. Half the city shall go forth into captivity, but the residue of the people shall not be cut off from the city." (Zechariah 14:1).

Today, we can see this refers to the Battle of the Arab States against Jerusalem in 1947 and 1948. The Old City was indeed taken. The houses were looted and the women raped. Half the city (the Old City) fell into the hands of the Arabs. But they failed to capture the rest of Jerusalem which was to become Israel's capital.

Zechariah goes on to say, "Then shall the Lord go forth and fight against those nations as when he fought in the day of battle, and his feet will stand upon the Mount of Olives to the east of Jerusalem . . . You will escape through the valley, for it will reach across to the city gate."

This is what happened in the 1967 war when the Jews recaptured the Old City and East Jerusalem, reunifying the city. The attack did come from the east. The Israeli soldiers hooked around behind Jerusalem, going up onto the Mount of Olives. From that position they attacked the walls of the Old City, not from the west, from the side of New Jerusalem, but from the east, at the gate that is closest to the Mount of Olives. Fulfilling Zechariah's prediction that the enemies of Israel would escape through the valley, fleeing as though from an earthquake, the Arab refugees fled to the Jordan Valley, crossing the Jordan River.

Time has not yet caught up to the rest of the prophecy. From this point onward, our interpretations must move more cautiously. I believe that the living waters which "shall go out of Jerusalem towards the east and toward the west" (Zachariah 14:8) refer to the flow of religious inspiration coming out of Jerusalem, influencing both the Western world and the Eastern world of China, India, and Japan. Verses twelve and fifteen refer to the Arab-Israeli war which may be the Final War of Gog. Finally in verse sixteen, Zechariah predicts there will be peace between Jews and Arabs, a Semitic union after the War of Gog. Then Jerusalem will be exalted as the holy city of Jews, Christians, and Moslems; and חג הסוכות the Feast of Sukkot (The Feast of Tabernacles) will be celebrated not only by the Jewish people but will spread throughout the nations.

It would be wrong to infer from this prediction that at the end of the Messianic Age, everyone will convert to Judaism. It is true that Zechariah forecasts, "Thus sayeth the Lord of Hosts, 'In those days it shall come to pass that ten men shall take hold. Out of the languages of the nations, shall even take hold of the shirt of him that is a Jew, saying, "we will go with you for we have heard that God is with you . . ." (8:23).

It seems likely that millions of people will convert to Judaism as the truth of the chosenness of the Jewish people becomes apparent. The prophet Isaiah predicted. "In the end of days (the culmination of the Messianic Age) it shall come to pass that the mountain of the Lord's house shall be established as the top of the mountains. It shall be exalted above the hills. And people shall flow unto it. Many nations shall go and say, come ye, let us go up to the mountain of the Lord, to the House of the God of Jacob. He will teach us his ways and we will walk in His paths. For out of Zion shall go forth the Torah, and Word of the Lord from Jerusalem" (Isaiah 2:2-3).

One cannot but feel that those who are firm in their faith during these difficult days, whether they came to Judaism by conversion or inheritance, are more praiseworthy than those who convert or show an awakening of enthusiasm after God's covenant with His people is clearly confirmed. But this is only an aside. More importantly, even in the end of days, there will be no universal conversion to Judaism.

The most popular of all the prophecies referring to the culmination of the Messianic Age, the ימות המשיח *Ymot Hamoshe'ah,* the reign of universal peace and justice, appears twice in the Bible, once from the lips of Isaiah and once from the prophet Micah: "He (referring to God) shall judge between many peoples and shall decide concerning mighty nations far off. They shall beat their swords into plowshares and their spears into pruning hooks. Nation shall not lift up sword against nation, neither shall they learn to make war any more" (Isaiah 2:3 Micah 4:3).

Micah goes on with his vision to make a very important point: "Let all the peoples walk, each one in the name of its God, we will walk in the name of the Lord our God forever" (Micah 4:5).

There is only one God. But there is more than one true religion. The Jews do not believe that they alone of all mankind have the only access to God. For this reason there are no Jewish missionaries. We believe there are many paths to God, and many ways to worship the Infinite. People's manner of relating to the Infinite depends upon their culture, their family, and their own personality. We welcome those who wish to follow our path, but we respect those who follow different paths. The only essential behavior for all human beings is to execute justice and righteousness, to love mercy, and to take care of the weak.

Universal justice and peace cannot be created by forcing everyone to be alike, by converting everyone to a single belief, or by assimilating everyone to a single cultural style. There are hundreds of different human languages.

All of them are adequate for communicating the needs and desires of their own peoples. No language is superior to all the others. In the same way, each culture has its own unique genius, its own special ways of expressing human life: This diversity of religion, of culture, of nationality, of language, is precious. It is beloved of God.

Will we ever reach the stage when people will be able to respect one another, not because they share common values and interests, but because they differ in beliefs and behavior? The Messianic Hope says yes. If so, why is it necessary for Israel and the rest of mankind to pass through the military, political, and social upheavals of the חבלי המשיח Hevlay Hamoshe'ah, the birthpangs, of the Messianic Age?

In truth, we might be able to escape the Hevlay Hamoshe'ah if we by ourselves repent. But if we don't repent, could mankind really be doomed to destruction? Would God let man destroy mankind? Wouldn't He redeem us from ultimate destruction even if we don't repent?

There is recorded in the Talmud (Sanhedrin 97b) a very interesting controversy, in the form of a debate, between two disciples of Rabban Johanan ben Zakkai, Rabbi Eliezer ben Hyrcanus and Rabbi Joshua ben Hananiah, both of whom began their careers before the destruction of the Temple. The point at issue between them was whether repentance is an indispensable prerequisite of redemption or not:

Rabbi Eliezer taught: If Israel repent, they will be redeemed, as it is written (Jer. 3:22), "Return, ye backsliding children, I will heal your backslidings." Rabbi Joshua said to him: But is it not written (Isa. 52:3): — "Ye have sold yourselves for nought, and ye shall be redeemed without money: — "Ye have sold yourselves for nought," i.e. for idolatry; "And ye shall be redeemed without money," i.e. without repentance and good deeds? Rabbi Eliezer retorted to Rabbi Joshua: But is it not written (Mal. 3:7), "Return unto Me, and I will return unto you"? Rabbi Joshua answered: But is it not written (Dan. 12:7),"And I heard the man who swore by Him that it ?th forever, that it shall be for a time, times, and a half; and when they have made an end of breaking in pieces the power of the holy people, all these things shall be consummated" (hence there is a determined end, even if Israel does not repent?) At this Rabbi Eliezer remained silent.

Rabbi Joshua ben Hananiah won the argument. God will redeem his people, and all of mankind, in His own time, even if we don't repent. Of course repentance will hasten the process and bring the "end." Yet worthy or not, God will not allow the Jewish people to be destroyed, or mankind to perish. However, Rabbi Eliezer found a good reply to Rabbi Joshua.

Rabbi Eliezer said: If Israel repent, they will be redeemed; if not, they will not be redeemed. Rabbi Joshua said to him: If they do not repent, will they not be redeemed? (impossible) Rabbi Eliezer replied: The Holy One, blessed be He, will set up over them a king, whose decrees shall be as cruel as Haman's; then Israel will repent, and He will bring them back to their own land.

This statement is listed first in the text but it must have come about after Rabbi Eliezer was silenced by Rabbi Joshua's quote from Daniel showing that there would be a redemption when a fixed (and unknown to us) stage had been reached. Eliezer still believed in the power of spiritual repentance. Eliezer was an idealist and a strong believer in free will. Eliezer (his name means "my God helps") believed that humans must do something to merit God's help. This means that if we fail, we could be destroyed. Joshua believes that God will not let humanity perish because it would be against his nature i.e. his goodness and love. Eliezer's solution is that God will trap us into Repentance (just as God did in the Garden of Eden with the Serpent). Until the Final Day—the Kaytz, קץ the end of days, our voluntary repentance is the primary factor.

A story in the Talmud illustrates his position: Rabbi Yehoshuah ben Levi had a vision in which he spoke to the Messiah, asking him when he would come to deliver the Jewish people. "Today," the Messiah told him. But that day passed and was no different from any other day. Feeling betrayed, Rabbi Yehoshuah ben Levi complained to Elijah that the Messiah had lied to him. But Elijah replied, "The Messiah would indeed have come today if only everybody listened to God's voice." In other words any date could be the date for redemption: God has the patience to wait until human nature matures sufficiently to live according to God's will. Then, we will have achieved the Messianic promise.

Rabbi Joshua was less sanguine about his species. Humans change, he suspected, only when forced by grim circumstance. His confidence rested in God . He believed God would provide stalled humanity with the needed boost by allowing circumstances to become sufficiently grim to evoke change. In Joshua's model of redemption "the end" קץ the *Kaytz* will be more the result of God's push, than our pull.

Joshua and the other realists fear maturation will never be achieved by human power alone. To change sufficiently, they feel, humanity requires the catalyst of cataclysmic events. Tremendous upheavals create suffering. Suffering stimulates spiritual growth. When the upheavals cause sufficient suffering to stimulate sufficient spiritual growth, humanity will finally repent, ushering in the culmination of the Messianic Age.

Although the two sages seem to have differing views, both saw clearly. If humanity voluntarily gives up its materialism and selfishness, and learns to live in righteousness and compassion, for the sake of human dignity and the love of God, there will be no birth agonies preceding the Messianic Age, but rather, a steady improvement in the human social and spiritual condition. However, God will not fail us. If we are unable to spark our own moral evolution, he will allow a sequence of catastrophes to fall upon us, and God will force us to struggle out of the conflict and chaos into the new age.

These two visions differ in the means but not the final outcome. The new age for humanity is certain in both. There is a third view of the future, the dark foreboding of the pessimists. They believe humanity will never be redeemed. They see overpopulation, ecological disaster, or nuclear war as our final destiny. These pessimists offer no hope for the human race. This belief is a product of disgust, impatience with human imperfection, and lack of courage to persevere in a difficult path. The various interpretations of the Messianic Promise differ only between the idealists and the realists. Pessimism is rejected by all. The Jewish vision of history has an ending, not with a bang, nor with a whimper, but with a triumph.

No Jew who believes in God can be a pessimist concerning human destiny. It is currently very fashionable to disparage humanity and our efforts. People point to all of the negative aspects of civilization and technology. They take for granted all that has been accomplished by diligent effort, and by people who had confidence that problems could be solved. Diseases could be vanquished. Nature could be tamed. And society can be made just and peaceful. We need to believe firmly in the Messianic Age or we will not have the conviction and energy to sustain our efforts to realize it. This is especially true during periods of social-political upheaval and rapid technological change.

The majority of rabbinic projections concerning the Messianic Age are based on the cataclysmic model. The first part of the Messianic Age, the period of chaos and suffering is called the חבלי המשיח Hevlay Hamoshe'ah, the birthpangs of the Messiah. That phrase itself suggests the realists' point of view: Just as humans cannot come into existence without the struggle of birth, so the Messianic culmination can be created only through labor and travail.

When people are told that a coming event will transform their lives, they naturally want to know when it will occur. So it has been with the realistic view of the Messianic culmination. Ever since the predictions first were made of an age of justice and truth preceded by a time of chaos, there were those who hoped ... and predicted ... every time the Western world suffered a spate of bad times, the חבלי המשיח the *Hevlay Hamoshe'ah,* the birthpangs of the Messianic Age had begun, and the golden age was on the horizon.

With such a long history of faulty prediction behind us, how can we dare fix the dates ot the Messianic unfolding? Only because the ingathering of the Jewish people, that recurrent theme among the prophecies, has finally occured during our lifetime.

The ingathering of the dispersed Jewish people to their ancient homeland was the most frequently mentioned event signaling the beginning of the Messianic Age. Isaiah foretold, "On that day, the Lord will set his hand again, a second time, by recovering the Remnant of his people, those who are still left, from Assyria and Egypt, from Pathros, from Ethiopia and Elam, from Shinar, Hamath, and the islands of the sea. Then he will raise a signal to the nations and gather those driven out of Israel. He will assemble Judah's scattered people from the four corners of the earth" (Isaiah 11:11-12).

Jeremiah who was active in the decades preceding the destruction of Jerusalem and the Babylonian exile (both of which he forecast) spoke of a return within a period of seventy years: "These are the words of the Lord, 'When a full seventy years has passed over Babylon, I will take up your cause and fulfill the promise of good things I made you by bringing you back to this place' "(Jeremiah 29:10).

This prophecy like many of Jeremiah's other prophecies refers to the first ingathering of the dispersed Jewish people which occured in the year 537 BCE, and culminated in the rebuilding of the Temple and the establishment of the second Jewish commonwealth. Indeed, the prophets who spoke before the Babylonian exile create a problem for scholars who must sort out which of their passages refer to the ingathering that precedes the Messianic Age, and which refer to the return from Babylonia.

Fortunately, this problem does not exist with the words of the prophets who lived after the return from the Babylonian exile. Zechariah prophesied "in the fourth year of Darius" about twenty years after the return from Babylonia. His prophecies cover a period of thirty to forty years, beginning with the rebuilding of the Temple which had commenced shortly before the year 520 BCE. In the Torah, the first eight chapters of Zechariah are concerned mainly with issues of his own day, but the last six (9—14) consisting of prophecies made about 480 BCE, clearly apply to the final ingathering as part of the Messianic fulfillment. Zechariah delivers the message of the Lord: "See, I will rescue my people from the countries of the east and the west and bring them back to live in Jerusalem. They shall be My people and I will be their God in truth and justice." (Zechariah 8:7-8).

Troubles we have always had—war, social change, and civil unrest. But never before in the twenty-seven hundred years since the Messianic vision began to form have two such unmistakable signs occurred: the ingathering of the exiles to the Land of Israel, and the restoration of the Jewish state. This is a very strong indication that we are living in the חבלי המשיח *Hevlay Hamoshe'ah*, the Birthpangs of the Messiah and therefore, we are in a better position to understand the significance of the visions and prophecies than those who have tried before us.

The most exciting of these prophecies are to be found in the Rabbinic literature. But since Christians as well as Jews are interested in interpreting the prophecies of the Messianic Age, I shall use the *Book of Daniel*, which is common to both religions, as the basis of my calculations.

Daniel says of his visionary dream, ". . . I saw a great storm on a mighty ocean, with strong winds blowing from every direction. Then huge animals came up out of the water, each different from the other. The first was like a lion, but it had eagle's wings. And as I watched, its wings were pulled off so that it could no longer fly, and it was left standing on the ground, on two feet, like a man; and a man's mind was given to it. The second animal looked like a bear with its paw raised, ready to strike. It held three ribs between its teeth, and I heard a voice saying to it, 'Get up! Devour many people!' The third of these strange animals looked like a leopard, but on its back it had four heads! And great power was given to it over all mankind. Then as I watched in my dream, a fourth animal rose up out of the ocean, too dreadful to describe and incredibly strong. It devoured some of its victims by tearing them apart with huge iron teeth, and others it crushed beneath its feet. It was far more brutal and vicious than any of the other animals." (Daniel 7:2-7).

Daniel was very much afraid of what he had seen so he asked the personages in his dream what it meant. He was told that these great beasts represent four kingdoms which shall arise from the earth. The fourth beast represented the fourth kingdom which would be radically different and more brutal than all those before it. "The fourth beast shall be a fourth kingdom, different from all the other kingdoms and shall devour the whole earth and shred it down and break it into pieces." (Daniel 7:23) Following the fourth kingdom, Daniel was told, the Ancient of Days will come with his court to judge and vindicate his people. Then every nation under heaven, and all their power, shall be given forever to the people who obey God.

Daniel's visionary dream of hope has stimulated countless attempts to indentify the four kingdoms. During the medieval period the Church supported the widespread belief that the beasts symbolized Babylonia, Persia, Greece, and Rome. Referring to itself during this period as the Holy Roman Empire, successor to the secular empire of the Romans, the Church hoped to be, or at the very least hoped to be thought of, as representing God's rule on earth. Conditions on earth after the Church of Rome's establishment failed to conform to Daniel's vision of justice and peace. Even the theory was weak in that civilization under the Romans was much the same as it had been under the Greeks before them. The error of almost all commentators on Daniel has been to link each beast to one political unit such as a kingdom or an individual empire.

A striking clue to the identity of the first beast is that it touched Daniel and his seed. This characteristic could only apply to the Semitic culture expressed in the Babylonian-Assyrian-Persian empires which formed in the Middle East during a stretch of centuries ranging roughly from 1750 to 333BCE. The length of time may seem impossibly long to symbolize one unit to our twentieth century eyes, but we must remember that change occurred at an almost imperceptible rate in pre-industrial civilizations. Studying the art of these three empires will provide evidence of their essential unity in a most pleasant fashion.

The second kingdom was the Greco-Macedonian-Roman civilization. Here, too, despite a shifting of power from one geographic region to another , one language to another, and across a span of eight to ten centuries, a basic Hellenistic culture unified the entire achievement.

The third beast symbolized the Moslem civilization. Emerging from a Semitic culture, the Moslems came into power in the Middle East and burst into North Africa, Spain, and southern Europe.

Finally, the fourth and most terrifying kingdom is the civilization of Christian Western Europe. The industrial revolution provided the technology for this civilization's eventual domination of almost the entire world, calling to mind the huge devouring iron teeth of the beast in Daniel's dream. Indeed this civilization meets the criterion of being radically different from those before it.

Now let's use our indentification of the four kingdom as a basis for working out a timetable for predicting the arrival of the Messianic Age. A number of periods of time are given in the Book of Daniel. Four are specific, one is conjectural. Daniel mentions 2300 evenings and mornings. (9:14) He also speaks of 1290 days; and in the next verse, he mentions 1335 days (12:11-12). His fourth specific period is 490 years (9:24).

Additionally, he mentions time, times and a half (12:7). In the language of his day this means 1 (time) + 2(times) + $\frac{1}{2}$, equalling $3\frac{1}{2}$. But Daniel leaves to our ingenuity to discover three and a half what. One of the leading commentators on the Book of Daniel, Rabbi Abarbanel, believed the mysterious factor to be the length of time that the first Temple was devoted to the worship of the Lord, or $3\frac{1}{2}$ times 410 years, or 1435 years. I believe his interpretation is correct.

Historians generally agree that the Persian empire, the last of the Babylonian-Assyrian-Persian triumverate, came to an end in the year 333 BCE when the Persian army was defeated by Alexander the Great of Macedon in the Battle of Issus. Of course, Greek civilization had been incubating for several centuries before this battle, but taking 333 BCE as the date marking the end of the first civilization and the emergence of the second as a major world power, we can work out the following equation: 2300 (Daniel 8:14) less 1335 (Daniel 12:12) equals 965. If we add 965 to the year 333 BCE we arrive at the year 632 of the common era.

Mohammed died in 632. At that time the Greco-Roman civilization was collapsing of its own weight, leaving political chaos in Europe. Shortly after Mohammed's death, the Arabs began their invasion of the Middle East, Iran, Egypt, North Africa, and the Byzantine Empire. For the next seven or eight centuries, while Europe groped through the dark ages, the Moslem world was the center of western civilization, covering a stretch of territory from Spain in the west to Persia in the east.

The date of the next shift in world empire can be found by taking 1335 and adding to it 490 (Daniel 9:24). This gives us the sum 1825 which, when added to 333 BCE brings us to the year 1492; Europe's discovery of America. Rapid exploration, conquest, and occupation followed. Fourteen hundred and ninety-two marks the begining of the great European colonial empires, the begining of the great mercantile empires, and the dawn of industrialization. Fourteen hundred and ninety-two also dates the expulsion of the Jews from Spain and the fall of Granada, the last Moslem stronghold in Spain. Islam's power was weakening and the new voracious Christian countries of western Europe were moving toward their eventual world domination.

You might think we still live in the period of ascendancy of the kingdom of Christian European civilization, but our calculations suggest otherwise. Using Daniel's figures for the prediction of the ending of this kingdom, we take 1435 (Daniel 12:7 as interpreted by Abarbanel) and to that add 1335, 1290, and 490, equaling 4550. From 4550 we subtract 2300, and when we add the result to 333BCE, we obtain 1917.

Four Beast / Kingdom Chart

Kingdom Old and New	Beginning and End	Daniels Calculations
Old—Lion with Eagle wings Babylonia/Assyria/Persia	Genesis 11:10-30	2300 −1335
		965 −333
New—Greek/Roman	333 BCE	632
Old—Devouring Bear Greece—Rome	333 BCE	1335 +490
		1825 −333
New—Islamic	632 CE	1492
Leopard with four heads Old—Islamic Empire Omayyads—Abbasids Mamluks and Turks	632 CE	1435 +1335 +1290 + 490
		4550 −2300
		2250 − 333
New—Western Europe	1492 CE	1917
Christian Colonialist Europe Spain, England, France, Germany The Messianic Age	1492 CE 1917 CE	The coming of the Ancient of Days ?

Nineteen hundred and seventeen is the date of the United States' entry into World War I, marking the beginning of this country's worldwide military and political power. It was the date of the revolution in old Russia, culminating in the victory and spread of communism. And perhaps most significantly, it was the date of the Balfour Declaration when the British officially recognized the right of the Jewish people to establish themselves in the Land of Israel. Indeed, 1917 does seem to be a boundary date, the end of one era, the beginning of the another. The beginning of the long awaited, much dreaded *Hevlay Hamoshe'ah,* the Birthpangs of the Messianic Age.

The objective data which sustains my belief in the essential rightness of these mystical interpretations center around the conclusion that ours is an age that is significantly different than those that came before it.

Never before has humanity developed the technology to do away with itself. We have had wars before, horrible wars. Cities have been sacked, countrysides wasted, and great chunks of a population killed off. But in the past, limitations of weapons and means of transportation, confined the scope of wars. While one community of nations busied itself destroying each other, somewhere two or three thousand miles away, another culture was creatively developing.

Human history is a record of one culture dying out or being dispached, while elsewhere others were progressing, moving ahead, gaining in population, and often even able to save much of the knowledge and arts of another decaying civilization.

Today, we are confronted by the technical possibility that the next war could be the last ... the last for all of us. Even the underdeveloped countries are dependent on international trade for tools, energy and medicine. The destruction of the advanced countries will also doom them.

Many scientists feel that our greatest danger as a civilization and a species is not nuclear warfare but the destruction of our environment and the exhaustion of the planet's natural resources. Until the last two or three centuries, the human population though growing out of proportion to other predatory life forms, was not pressing the planet's capacity to support it. Disease, famine, natural catastrophes, and to a lesser extent, war fatalities kept our numbers manageable.

Now human technology in agriculture and medicine has tipped the balance. Our population is expanding so rapidly we are fouling the earth's water, contaminating and destroying its atmosphere, stripping the earth of its natural resources, and killing off its life forms to an extent that alarms ecologists and biologists. Increasing numbers of scientists from a variety of disciplines add their voices to the warning that if we humans don't learn to govern ourselves by limiting our population, limiting our consumption of energy and materials, and learn to use long range environmental planning, we risk destroying the earth's capacity to support us.

This is a radical new factor in human history. It is one that affects every nation and people.

The third factor, the return of the Jews to their homeland and the establishment of an independent state, fulfilling the Messianic predictions, has already been discussed. Thus three radical developments make our generation the first to face the challange of the new age.

Other prophecies have also been fulfilled, more than there is space for in this book, far less in a single chapter. For me they add up to one conclusion: We are actually living through the birthpangs of the Messianic Age, the *Hevlay Hamoshe'ah*. The Messianic Age is at hand.

So far I have scarcely referred to the Messiah. The reason is that the Age is more important than the agent. The Messiah is simply an agent of God who helps bring about the new world. In reality it is the partnership of God and humanity that will achieve the culmination of the Messianic Age. The Bible records a number of instances in which God spoke of bringing about this age without mentionong his anointed agent. The prophets Nahum, Zephaniah, Joel, Habakkuk, and Malachi, speak also of the age without mentioning a Messiah. There are references to more than one Messianic deliverer, or saints or shepherds, as they are sometimes called, in the books of Amos, Ezekiel, and Obadiah.

Historical events are brought about by people. Leaders are essential to articulate the needs of their age and the feeling of their followers, and to organize and direct action. But leaders can accomplish nothing by themselves. We say that Napoleon invaded Russia. But he did not charge into Russia alone; he led an army. Mahatma Gandhi did not bring about independence for India by himself; nor did Theodore Herzl create the State of Israel by himself. Followers are essential. This fact lies behind the statement that people cannot blame their country's corruption on their leaders. Without followers, a leader is just a single person going nowhere.

Everyone can become a Messianic figure. Everyone's participation is needed.

But who will be our leader? Who is the Messiah to be?

The prophets say the Messiah will be a descendant of King David. David was the greatest king of Israel, a military leader who defeated the enemies of the Jewish people, a man who, despite his faults, took the Lord to heart and sought to do as well as he could, a musician and a poet who composed songs of praise and danced before the Ark of the Lord.

Limiting the selection of the Messiah to a descendant of David implies little more than stipulating the Messiah will be of Jewish birth. One hundred generations have been born since David lived, families marrying into families. Those Jewish families who have kept careful lineages find that the House of David has often entered their family tree at one point or another over the centuries. If accurate records had been kept as they were in Biblical days, the overwhelming majority of the Jewish people would find they could trace their ancestry back to the famous King of Israel.

"There shall come forth," the prophet Isaiah predicted, "a twig out of the stock of Jesse (the father of David). A twig shall grow forth out of his roots. And the spirit of the Lord shall rest upon him, the spirit of wisdom and understanding, the spirit of counsel and might, the spirit of knowledge, and the fear of the Lord. His delight shall be in the fear of the Lord. He shall not judge after the sight of his eyes nor decide after the hearing of his ears. But with righteousness shall he judge the poor and decide with equity for the meek of the land (Isaiah 11:1-4).

Several verses later the prophet says, "It shall come to pass in that day that the root of Jesse (that is, the Messiah) will stand for an ensign for the people and unto him the nations shall seek." Isaiah foresaw that ". . . the Lord shall gather in the Jewish people from the various places where they have been scattered and will set up the ensign for the nations and assemble the dispersed of Israel from the four corners of the earth" (11:10-12).

When I was in Jerusalem in 1974, I learned a Kabbalistic insight about the coming of the Messiah. There are two major Messianic figures: the Messiah, the son of David and the Messiah, the son of Joseph. This concept is part of the rabbinic tradition as well as of the Kabbalists'. Just as the original Joseph became a ruler in the land of Egypt for the Jews living outside of Israel, so the Messiah, the son of Joseph, will be a leader of the Jews living outside the Land of Israel, while the Messiah, the son of David, would come forth from within the Land of Israel.

In August 1897 Theodore Herzl convened the first session of the World Zionist Congress in Basel, Switzerland. At the close of that convention, Herzl wrote in his diary, "If I were to sum up the congress in a word, it should be this: At Basel, I founded the Jewish State. If I said this out loud today, I would be greeted with universal laughter. In five years perhaps, and certainly in fifty years, everyone will perceive it."

Exactly fifty years later, in August of 1947, the Special Commission of the United Nations on Palestine recommended the partition of Palestine and the establishment of a Jewish State. This amazing fulfillment of Herzl's prophecy strongly suggests that Theodore Herzl, a leader who lived outside the Land of Israel, is a Messianic figure. Not the Messiah, the son of David, but his forerunner, the Messiah, the son of Joseph.

What does this say about the Messiah, the son of David? Isaiah saw the Messiah as a Jew who would play a major role in the ingathering of the Jewish people into the Land of Israel, a great leader who will be a righteous judge.

The prophet Jeremiah believed the Messiah would become more powerful than a common leader: "Behold the day comes, says the Lord, when I will raise unto David a righteous shoot. He shall reign as king and prosper and shall execute justice and righteousness in the land" (Jeremiah 23:5).

God will do this for God acts in history by inspiring people.

Thus the Messiah is God's agent in leading Israel and the world into the Messianic Age. God, not the Messiah, is crucial to redemption. God's intervention will be to encourage human growth and human participation. Spiritual growth must be developed, human participation must come, if we are to realize the Messianic promise. The culmination of the Messianic Age is not a birthday present that God will give to humanity. It is a goal humanity can achieve in partnership with God, when we struggle vigilantly and persistently, without despairing over our obstacles or becoming complacent over our successes.

We can hasten the coming of the Messianic Age and therefore shorten the period of the *Hevlay Hamoshe'ah*. We have already begun to experience the first waves of catastrophes. Let's hope we will not need many more. The upheavals some of the prophets foresaw are terrible to contemplate. More than once in the Talmud it was said, "May the Messiah come, but not in my lifetime."

In 1917, the Balfour Declaration was issued. Thirty years later, in 1947, the United Nations voted to establish a Jewish State in the Land of Palestine, and twenty years after that, in 1967 the City of Jerusalem, which had been cut off as predicted by the prophet Zechariah, was reunited to Israel during the Six-Day War. In 1977 Sadat came to Jerusalem. The peace process begins.

A pattern emerges. Years ending in seven seem to have particular significance for the Messianic unfolding. The next stage (1987 or 1997) could be the year of the War of Gog or, if we successfully pass the test, it may be the beginning of the era of peace. Whether we have learned to make war or peace, the son of David may then come forward to lead us.

I speak these words with great hesitation for I know the Jewish tradition has condemned the attempt to calculate the end. Rabbi Yonatan says in the Talmud, "May all those who calculate the end perish, for men will say that since the predicted end is here and the Messiah is not here, he will never come."

It must be understood that humans are fallible. If indeed the interpretations we have made do not come to pass, it is not that God has abandoned His people, but that we have not adequately understood the nature of the times in which we live. In the Mekilta of Rabbi Simeon it is written, ". . . let a man wait and believe, and the good is bound to come."

Nevertheless, because so many people live in fear that the world will end in nuclear holocaust or environmental poisoning, because so many are searching frantically for some assurance that the Messianic Age is to be, and because so many well-meaning attempts are being made to interpret the Biblical prophecies of the Messianic Age by those who cannot read scripture in its original language, and so quickly fall into misinterpretation, I have felt a responsibility to speak out.

כִּי מִצִּיּוֹן תֵּצֵא תוֹרָה וּדְבַר יְיָ מִירוּשָׁלָם. וְשָׁפַט בֵּין עַמִּים רַבִּים וְהוֹכִיחַ לְגוֹיִם עֲצֻמִים עַד־רָחוֹק, וְכִתְּתוּ חַרְבֹתֵיהֶם לְאִתִּים, וַחֲנִיתֹתֵיהֶם לְמַזְמֵרוֹת, לֹא־יִשְׂאוּ גוֹי אֶל־גּוֹי חֶרֶב, וְלֹא־יִלְמְדוּן עוֹד מִלְחָמָה. וְיָשְׁבוּ אִישׁ תַּחַת גַּפְנוֹ וְתַחַת תְּאֵנָתוֹ וְאֵין מַחֲרִיד, כִּי־פִי יְיָ צְבָאוֹת דִּבֵּר. כִּי כָּל־הָעַמִּים יֵלְכוּ אִישׁ בְּשֵׁם אֱלֹהָיו, וַאֲנַחְנוּ נֵלֵךְ בְּשֵׁם־יְיָ אֱלֹהֵינוּ לְעוֹלָם וָעֶד.

"For *Torah* will go forth from Zion, and the word of the Lord from Jerusalem. He shall Judge between many nations, and rebuke mighty, even distant, nations. They shall beat their swords into plowshares and their spears into pruning knifes nation shall not lift up sword against nation neither shall they learn war any more. They shall sit, each man under his Vine and under his Fig Tree and no one shall make them afraid. For the mouth of the Lord of Hosts has spoken. So let all peoples walk each one in the name of its God we will walk in the name of YHVH our God for ever."

INTELLIGENT BEINGS IN OUTER SPACE

Do you believe there are intelligent life forms in outer space?
I do.

It is inconceivable to me that intelligent life exists only on one speck of dust circling a rather average star among 200 billion other stars in one of the millions of galaxies in this universe.

I predict we will contact, or be contacted by, intelligent beings from outer space in the next generation or two.

Until contact, I cannot prove my conviction, but I can show you how to estimate the probability that intelligent life exists somewhere out there in the vast and starry heavens, along with the probability that we will be able to communicate with them, and how this links up with a major Kabbalistic belief.

To calculate the probability of contacting extraterrestrial intelligent life, we'll use the formula devised by Professor Frank Drake of the Center for Radiophysics and Space Research at Cornell University. His equation contains seven major factors, the results of seven mathematical operations we will make to arrive at a statistical estimate of the probability that we will communicate with intelligent beings in outer space.

Our starting place, factor one, is the total number of stars in the universe at this time. Then, as there is no way that life as we know it could exist in the radiant energy of a star, for operation 2, we divide the total number of stars by the percentage of stars having planetary systems. The answer we obtain, we divide (operation 3) by the percentage of planets which are ecologically suitable for the development of life as we know it. That answer we divide (operation 4) by the percentage of planets on which life actually came into being. This answer we divide (operation 5) by the percentage of planets on which life evolved into a race of intelligent beings. This last answer we divide (operation 6) by the percentage of planets on which a civilization capable of communicating across space to other stars was developed. Finally, we must calculate (operation 7), the most difficult and important factor of all: the Messianic Age.

Before I explain the Messianic factor, let's look at the six factors relating to the physical universe.

If we insisted on an exact count to fill in the numbers for all the factors of this equation, we would have to wait for future developments in science. Astronomers have estimated the number of stars in the galaxy and the number of galaxies in the universe. How many of these stars have planetary systems? How many of those planets developed life? Astronomers don't know; they can't estimate. They can only make a wild guess on the basis of their present drabs of information.

In order to start using the equation now, let's plug in figures astronomers admit are only guesstimates. If you've found another set of figures than the one I'm using, use your set. In making calculations about the universe, a few million here or there, doesn't affect the final result significantly. What is critical is the last factor, the one relating to the Messianic Age.

Since the most solid figure we have is the 200 billion star estimate for our galaxy, I'm going to start with it, estimating the probability of contact with intelligent life from within our galaxy and then expand our results to include the universe. We begin, then, with the figure 200 billion. How many of those two hundred billion stars have planetary systems of their own?

We don't know, but astronomers believe that planetary systems are not rare in the formation of a galaxy. The favored theory for the making of planets is: In the early stages of a galaxy's development, immense clouds of hydrogen gas slowly condense into the giant balls of fissioning matter we call stars. Within the hydrogen clouds are local eddies of condensing gas containing minute particles of heavy elements. These elements were left over from the explosion shattered corpses of stars born, burned, and exploded while the universe was younger still. At this later date some of the minute fragments of the rubble from their explosion fail to fall into the nearby developing star and instead gravitate together and eventually become planets.

The fact that our star, the sun, has at least nine planets would seem to back up the theory that planets are plentiful in our galaxy. If our star had only one or two planets, we would be more likely to feel the formation of planets was rare. Similarly, the fact that many planets in our solar system have smaller satellites—moons—of their own, adds weight to the argument.

At present, the sole method astronomers have to try to discover planets outside our solar system is to focus their telescopes on binary stars—two stars—revolving around a common center of gravity. Any irregularities in the revolutions of these twins from a mathematical model of what their revolution should be, makes scientists suspect the existence of a small, dark body in their vicinity. So, although astronomers can't actually see planets, which don't radiate light except faintly by reflection, they can infer their presence by the wobble of one or both of the binary twins.

A planet's gravitational pull is proportionate to its relatively small size so even a giant planet like Jupiter could cause only a slight wobble in a star's revolving path through space. Of course, the slighter the wobble, the harder it is to detect. Binary stars are rare in the portion of our galaxy near enough for telescopic study. Many of the binaries astronomers have found are so distant, they can't decide definitely whether their revolutions wobble or not.

Nevertheless, there is one twin—Bernard's star—close enough to expose a wobble in its revolution to the satisfaction of astronomers. The size and shape of its wobble suggests one of the stars has a planet of a size similar to our planets Jupiter or Saturn. When at last astronomers are able to view the planet through a telescop, perhaps in a space ship in orbit around the earth, we will have substantial proof that another planet exists in the galaxy besides those in our solar system. Possibly two others; for one astronomer has produced a set of calculations suggesting that Bernard's star has two planets rather than one giant planet.

Since at present we have no hard evidence for other galactic planets, let's assume for the sake of caution they are relatively rare in our galaxy, so that only one out of ten stars has at least one planet. Dividing the 200 billion stars in our galaxy by 1/10, we obtain 20 billion planet-circling stars for our second factor.

For factor three we need to decide how many of those 20 billion solar systems are ecologically suitable for the development of life as we know it. Life on earth is based on a chemistry of hydrogen and carbon. Theoretically life could develop from other chemical compositions. Perhaps life ferments in environments we now consider impossibly hostile for its development. However, continuing with a conservative approach, we'll limit ourselves not only to life based on hydrocarbons, but life based on water. In addition to the proper chemicals, hydrogen and oxygen, a water bearing planet must maintain a favorable distance from its star so that most of its surface temperatures most of the time will be neither so hot as to make water boil off in steam or so cold as to freeze it. In our solar system only one planet meets that requirement. A fact that heightens the probability that we have no neighbors in our solar system.

Rather than using the known percentage of waterbearing planets in our solar system (1/9), let's use a more conservative percentage, 1/100. Dividing 20 billion solar systems, which might have an average of 5 or 10 planets each by 500 or 1,000, or simply one each i.e. 20 billion planets by

100, we obtain an estimate of 200,000,000 water-bearing planets for our third factor.

Factor four requires an exciting consideration: How many of our galaxy's planets actually developed life? There have been a number of experiments which have sought to replicate the chemical composition of our atmosphere in its early days—three or four billion years ago—trying to reproduce the sun's radiation, thunderstorms' electric discharges, and all the other conditions of the young planet. The results have been the formation of simple amino acids in the laboratory. Amino acids are the component parts of protein, a major ingredient in the structure of cells, the primary unit of life. These experiments demonstrate that organic compounds will develop accidentally from inorganic chemicals. Of course, the chance of the transition occuring at any one time or specific place is hundreds of billions to one. But time was not in short supply in the development of our planet.

It took several hundred million years before the first signs of life did appear on this planet. Some estimates say longer, almost a billion years. More likely than not there were plenty of false starts before the final success. Early combinations of chemicals that did not work out. Amino acid chains that never formed into proteins. Proteins that never clustered into cell-like organizations. Cells that actually moved and nourished themselves, but died before they could reproduce, or reproduced so poorly there is no record of their existence. The point is despite the enormous stretch of time, despite the many failures in the process, finally earth developed a successful chain of life which eventually resulted in us.

Carl Sagan, the director of the Laboratory for Planetary Studies at Cornell University has stated, "Since we know of no special conditions on the primitive earth which could not be repeated on millions of other planets throughout the Galaxy, I have the sense, the feeling, that the origin of life is a very likely event. We already know that some kinds of meteorites have amino acids and large quantities of other organic compounds. We have good reason to think that comets have many organic compounds. There is now a large and rapidly expanding volume of evidence that a variety of organic compounds are produced in interstellar space, including CO (carbon monoxide), HCN (hydrogen cyanide), CH_3CN (acetonitrile), HCHO (formaldehyde), CH_3CHO (acetaldehyde), and HC_2CN (a compound rarely found on earth), particularly in dense clouds."

To continue with our conservative approach let's say that of the one percent (one out of a hundred) Galactic planets with the right environmental conditions for the development of simple life forms, only half actually did produce life. Personally, I believe life eventually develops on all planets environmentally suitable, because I have faith in God who is a life favorer.

Halving our estimate of 200 million planets capable of producing life leaves us with 100 million life-bearing planets by factor four. Since the galaxy contains 200 billion stars, the odds are 2,000 to one aginst any particular star having a solar system with even simple forms of life. The planets of all our neighboring stars could be barren even though the galaxy as a whole teems with life.

For factor five, we must decide how many life-bearing planets will develop intelligent, self conscious beings. If earth's example is normal, evolution from life to intelligent life is slower and chancier than from inorganic matter to life. It took less than a billion years for our planet to develop life, but it took three or four times that long to evolve only one species of symbol-using self conscious beings.

Had aliens from outer space been observing earth, coming by every million years or so, they would have visited earth three or four thousand times without finding intelligent creatures. Not until the last two or three visits would they have been able to observe intelligent humans.

Since humans were so long in coming, and since they came alone, we must assume that intelligent self awareness is not common in evolution. It may be a rather unusual development, rarely found in our galaxy.

Some scientists are more optimistic, pointing to several considerations. It's possible that earth was abnormally slow in its rate of developing intelligence. Several anthropologists and zoologists believe that even on earth humans are flattering themselves with the belief they have a monopoly on intelligence. Dolphins and whales have fine, big brains, even proportionate to their size. They may be intelligent, self-aware, and able to communicate with one another, in which case, the emergence of intelligence life on earth would have to be pushed back to an earlier time.

Of couse, lacking hands, they have no technology and so can't fulfill factor six, whether or not they are intelligent. Another possibility is that our ancestor's territorial spread may have driven out another species, possibly a cousin primate, which had they remained in a favorable environment, might have developed intelligence. Or we may have killed off other intelligent species altogether; certainly something happened to Neanderthal Man. Perhaps if our race had been less aggressive, we might have had intellectual peers.

Difficult as it is to assing a numerical value to the possibility of intelligent life evolving, for the sake of going forward in our calculations, let's arbitrarily say that for factor five only one of a thousand life-bearing planets succeeds in producing intelligent, self-conscious beings. Dividing 100 million life-bearing planets by 1,000 gives us 100,000 planets in the galaxy with intelligent beings.

Factor six requires an estimate of the percentage of these planets whose intelligent beings build a civilization with the technical ability to send and receive communications across the vast distances of interstellar space.

We have yet to develop that ability ourselves, and the problems are of a complexity as vast as the distances between the stars. The speed of light, the fastest speed we have discovered, is 186,000 miles a second. Sending a message to a civilization on a planet some 200 light years away would take two hundred years.

Two hundred years to send a message, two hundred years to receive a reply; four hundred years for the exchange of a single message — twice the age of our nation! Imagine trying to communicate with a civilization existing tens of thousands of light years distance... and the majority of our galaxy's stars are that far away or farther.

Still, we can see ahead to the day when we will solve the difficulties and establish communication with alien planets, not perhaps as individuals but certainly civilization to civilization. At this moment scientists are listening for radio signals from space and attempting to send radio signals out to space. The exploits of American and Russian space probes demonstrates the initial achievements of interplanetary travel. And a research team needs only governmental funds to begin work on a major device "project cyclops", to receive radio transmissions from outer space.

There seems to be a domino effect with technology. The beginnings of technology are unpretentious: The use of a stick to help pick up grubs, a stone or club to extend the arm's hitting range ends, perhaps inevitably, with us landing on the moon. But let's say only seventy-five percent — three out of four — of the planets that evolve intelligent beings became the homeland of a civilization that achieves interstellar communication. Dividing 100,000 planets with intelligent life by $\frac{1}{4}$ gives us 75,000 planets whose beings may develop a technology capable of sending messages across interstellar space.

The ability alone may not completely satisfy factor six. There is also an emotional factor. Will every civilization that can, want to, communicate with beings on alien planets?

Personally, I think they will. A high level of technology argues for the existence of curiosity, a sense of adventure, and the love of knowledge for its own sake. Certainly, most of our own important discoveries have come through pure research — someone hunting down some stray piece of information or trying to solve a problem just for wanting to know. Many students of learning ability believe that curiosity is part and parcel of intelligence. If this is true, then any species intelligent enough to be able to communicate with extraterrestial aliens would also be curious enough to want to do so. But continuing to the last with our conservative approach, again let's say that only three quarters of the planets whose beings can achieve a breakthrough in interstellar communication will want to enough to devote the materials and time necessary to achieve it. Dividing 75,000 planets by $\frac{3}{4}$ gives us over 50,000 planets whose beings have put their medium of exchange on line for the building of a Project Cyclops and its successor projects. Fifty thousand planets out of the 200 billion stars we began with gives us odds of four million to one against any particular star having a planet with a space age civilization.

If you think I have been overly generous, tipping the balance in favor of my own theories, put the odds higher by 10 or even 100 times, making it 400 million to one against any particular star hitting the jackpot. Even then, with odds of 400 million to one, among our galaxy's 200 billion stars, our calculations suggest 500 will shine on a space age civilization.

So much for our galaxy. The universe has *millions* of others. The prospect is awesome.

Without having struggled through these calculations, most Americans agree with me that the probability of intelligent beings existing elsewhere in our universe is high. A recent Gallup poll indicated that almost half the nation's population believes there are intelligent creatures in outer space.

One final factor remains to be considered in assessing our chances of contacting extraterrestrial life, the most crucial one of all—the Messianic factor: the life span of a civilization with a highly developed technology.

We don't know, of course. If we look to history for a model of our future, what we find does nothing to make us sleep better at night. Dozens of civilizations have sprung up, flowered brilliantly, withered, and died. The reason are difficult to identify, no doubt in each case numbers of factors were operating at once. From our distance in time and space, some seem to have been destroyed by enemies from without, others from internal rot; a few fell before natural disasters such as a prolonged drought. The most successful were victimized by their achievement, becoming too large to be efficiently administrated, or too rich and soft to make the hard choices that were later called for.

When those civilizations died, other peoples and other cultures replaced them. But today, our technology has developed weapons, which if used, could destroy not the civilization of the countries directly involved but all civilizations and, conceivably, the entire human race. Right now in our own lifetime, humanity is answering the question can we survive ourselves.

So the final factor is the length of time space age civilizations survive. We know that nothing lasts forever. Even the stars eventually die. Scanning the course of human history, more civilizations have already died than now exist.

It is reasonable to suspect that our own civilization, and those of alien races also will not last forever? Birth and death, creation and destruction seem an inevitable part of existence; it is hard to believe that any civilization will be exempt from the normal pattern.

But what is our lifespan? A pessimist might look at the world situation and claim there is serious doubt that we will survive to reach the twenty-third or twenty-fourth century. Some wonder if we will see the twenty-first century. An optimist, while agreeing that homo sapiens have overwhelming problems that must be solved if we are to survive, feels confident that the very problems will stimulate solutions for managing them, and that we as a civilization will reorganize ourselves into a society uniquely capable of satisfying both humanity's and the planet's needs.

Whether you yourself are an optimist or a pessimist, notice the importance of this issue to our equation. While according to our most pessimistic calculations, there are 500 planets which develop intelligent life, the age of our galaxy is so great that, if the life span of a civilization is only a few hundred to a few thousand years, these civilizations can come into being, reach a high level of technology, and die, in total isolation, millions of years before or after the other 499 (or so) civilizations exist. We could have had neighbors in our galaxy but none during the lifetime of homo sapiens on planet earth.

A billion sounds so like a million, it makes imagining just how ancient our galaxy is difficult. The Atlanta Journal published Lou Erickson's method for acquiring a feel for the difference between a million and a billion: A man gave his wife a million dollars, saying she could spend a thousand of it every day. Three years later, his gift had been used up. So, he gave her a billion dollars, again telling her she could spend a thousand dollars a day. This time his gift lasted three thousand years.

Our galaxy is about 20 billion years old. The first intelligent creatures may have evolved 5-10 billion years ago. If space age civilizations last only a few thousand years the chance of two of them existing at the same time during that 5 to 10 billion years would be very very small. *Unless space age civilizations have a life expectancy in the million of years, there is no possiblity of contact between them.*

If God has given the Messianic promise of ultimately achieving an age of international peace and justice to all intelligent beings then they, as well as we, have the hope of continuing onward through the millenium. How many we cannot estimate. The rabbis foresaw the end of the time of trials, the transitional phase of the Messianic Age; some placed it in units of centuries, others anticipating even longer time units. They all agreed that humanity would win through the time of troubles and reach another age, called the New Age or the Coming World; but none marked its duration. I believe the transitional phase of the Messianic Age will require several centuries, but the Coming World will last for an incomprehensible span of time.

We have looked at the problem of communicating with extraterrestrial beings from an anthropocentric point of view, wondering if there is someone "out there" for us to communicate with.

Now let's look at the problem from the perspective of the universe.

Our galaxy is not unusual. It is one of a cluster of eighteen galaxies. Hundreds of thousands of such clusters fill the universe, each composed of anywhere from a dozen to several hundred galaxies.

It seems reasonable to assume the Messianic promise does extend to all of the universe's intelligent races: As they build toward a space-age technology, they will enter a Messianic transition and, through coping with their crises, eventually reach an era of great spiritual development, their New Age.

Their society's basic social and technological problems will have been solved. The main thrust of their energies will be directed towards fulfilling their partnership with the Divine, by helping other civilizations and by achieving greater spiritual insights which will further their understanding both of the individual and the universe.

Eventually as each emerging civilization passes from its Messianic Age to its era of the New World, it contacts intelligent beings from a distant star. Many science fiction stories have been written about this first contact, usually in terms of hostility. Their authors are mistaken. They judge the future in terms of the present. The upheavals of the Messianic Age function as a proving ground. Those races who are too aggressive, too competitive, too destructive, too selfish, too materialistic to achieve a culture-wide spiritual uplifting will destroy themselves long before they develop the technical sophistication needed for interstellar and intergalactic flight.

Furthermore the first contact between races from different planets and different suns will take place not in the flesh, but through energy-based communications like radio or television. The vast distances separating the various star systems, and the even greater distances between galaxies, makes hit-and-miss searches for alien life by space ship impossibly costly in time and energy. Electromagnetic radiation travels at the speed of light and can be broadcast in a 360 degree direction. It is faster, easier, and more economic to explore electronically.

Physical contact will come long after the two alien cultures have established electronic communication. The technical problems to make physical contact, even when the destination is known, are of such an order of difficulty that we may be certain the contact will be made for the purpose of furthering knowledge, rather than for aggression, which could only be pointless.

We can hope that those races who do not survive their Messianic transition without devastating nuclear wars, will not destroy themselves completely. Perhaps only their civilizations will come crashing down, setting technology back centuries, perhaps a millenium. Hopefully, enough of the race itself would survive to begin the social evolution towards civilization again, a new civilization that would realize the promise of the Messianic Age.

Having successfully passed through their Messianic transition, once civilizations from different star systems finally do contact each other, they will begin exchanging knowledge, both technical and spiritual. Just as different cultures on earth today fertilize each other and stimulate each other, while retaining their separate identities, space age interchange will accelerate spiritual and technical progress. As time goes on, the first two communicating civilizations will contact others. A network of interstellar, and ultimately, intergalactic, civilizations will link up and continue to grow. Gradually each of the participants will acquire an almost total knowledge of everything within the network. Each unique newcomer entering the network will add yet more knowledge, while receiving an unestimable fund of spirituality and knowledge from the network.

Over the course of time, some of these individual civilizations within the network may pass away. It seems inevitable that even New World cultures cannot transcend the Divine formula of birth, flowering, and death. Eventually their stars and their galaxies will exhaust their energies.

Assuming that, for whatever reason, member civilizations of this network do die, their spiritual achievements—their music, history, drama, art and religious experiences — their essence as a culture, will have become part of the universal intelligence. So that even though the civilization disappears physically, its spiritual essence will remain as part of the on-going universal intelligence, which in this sense will be immortal. The individual unit may die, but the universal intelligence will continue. It is a process we see in our own bodies. Individual cells are continually dying, the body as an entity lives; our awareness of self remains unimpaired. In the same way the universal intelligence will continue as long as the universe continues to exist and evolve.

Let's look at the characteristic of the universal intelligence.

1. It is universal, a network extending from galaxy to galaxy throughout the universe.

2. The universal intelligence is for all practical purposes immortal. Its member civilizations may die, but the totality of the spiritual-intellectual content of the network remains intact.

3. The universal intelligence itself is without form. It is an entity, but an entity which has no shape.

4. To the individual beings of the member civilizations, no matter how intelligent, the universal intelligence cannot be completely comprehended.

5. The Universal intelligence is all-knowing in the sense that it knows everything possible to know within the network.

6. Since all the civilizations that are part of the universal intelligence have passed through their Messianic transition, they all are peaceful, just, compassionate, or in a word, good.

We speak of God as all-knowing, as omnipresent, as being immortal, as beyond human comprehension, as being spiritual — without body, shape, or form, and, most important, of being the greatest manifestation of goodness. All this the universal intelligence is.

Thus, the universal intelligence, the network of intertwined and interrelated intelligences throughout the galaxy and throughout the universe *is* the Supreme Being. Now let us look at this from the Kabbalistic point of view:

The Kabbalah says the אין סוף Ein Sof, the Infinite — the Universal Intelligence — had to limit itself in order for anything else to exist. Since it was all there was, in order to create a physical universe, it was necessary to constrict itself. In order for intelligent creatures to come into being, and to have the free choice to be moral or not, the Divine had to limit its ability to fill the universe with its own moral rules and understanding.

The result is צמצום tsimtsum, the Divine contraction. The Ein Sof, the infinite, voluntarily contracted into an infinitesimal point which contained, potentially, all the universe. At the moment when tsimtsum was completed, creation began.

The author of the Zohar knew nothing of modern cosmology. Yet we should not assume he was ignorant of reality. Written at least two centuries before Copernicus, the Zohar contains the following statement:

"The earth revolves in a circle like a ball; some of the inhabitants are below and some above. All the creatures differ in their looks in accordance with the change of the climate. There are places on earth where there is light when the opposite places are in the dark. In other words, there is day in one place when there is night in another. There is one place where the day lasts for almost the entire twenty-four hours, except for a very short time of darkness."

Here we have most of modern astronomical concepts of our planet — its sphericity, its rotation on an axis, the annual changes of the length of the day, and the variation of climatic conditions from area to area. The Kabblists also recognized mystically the earth's antiquity. Rabbi Issac of Akko, writing in the 14th century estimated the age of the universe at 18 billion years. According to modern astronomers about 18 to 20 billion years ago, all the universe was contained in an infinite pressure point. Then, the point, thousands of times smaller than a period on this page, exploded; radiating light and elementary particles. These subatomic particles in turn formed tremendous gas clouds of hydrogen and the expansion of the universe began.

As the universe expanded, the clouds of hidrogen gas slowly condensed into stars, clustering into galaxies. The expansion still continues. When the first planets, capable of bearing life did so, and that life slowly evolved until one of its forms reached the point of moral self-consciousness, the Divine dimension re-emerged within the physical universe. This may have taken 10 to 15 billion years. The Torah hints about this when it relates that plants with life were created before our sun (Genesis 1:9-15).

The expansion will go on until all the planets capable of achieving intelligent self-awareness, have fulfilled their potential; when all the universe's races who are capable of making it through the Messianic transition have linked up with the universal intelligence and become a functioning part of its being. Then the Ein Sof, the Infinite One will have been totally reconstituted. The original harmony and unity that existed when only God filled the empty void of pre-creation will have been reconstituted within a physical universe by the spiritual development of the living creatures who were created in the image of God.

The Divine will exist for a moment of eternity in total spiritual, moral, and physical harmony. Then the process may repeat itself. Once more, the process of tsimtsum may begin; the universe will crumble and gradually contract.

As the expansion required billions of years so will the contraction. From God's perspective, time has no significance. When tsimtsum has compressed the Divine into an infinitely minute point containing all that is, another explosion will occur. A new expansion of matter; a new set of stars, new galaxies, new planets, new life forms evolving toward new expressions of intelligence. They will reach out by the Divine instinct that is within them, towards spirituality and its material expressions, which will once again re-establish physical and spiritual harmony with the Divine.

It is impossible to know how many such expansions and contractions have occurred before ours for each new creation totally wipes out the existence of the previous one from our perspective, though not from God's.

The Talmud, declares God had created many worlds before this one and, then, destroyed them. Ours may not be the first creation but merely one of a series which has perhaps gone on for cycles beyond the comprehension of humans.

If the Kabbalistic perspective is true, we may be co! fident that within the next few centuries our race will successfully pass t.rough the Messianic transition and achieve the New Age. In the process, we will communicate with intelligent races in outer space. Eventually, it may take a thousand years, we become part of the universal Divine intelligence.

The inner meaning of the Garden of Eden story tells us humanity took on the image of God by acquiring moral knowledge of Good and Evil, but we are yet to become truly Godlike. Only by eating of the fruit of the Tree of Life, which is immortality, can we become Godlike. This is the Torah's first hint of the Messianic promise.

This promise is the crux of the goal of human life. We find echoes of that promise in other lands too, in both their oral and written literature. Usually the promise is held to be a sacred part of their religious tradition. Its frequent appearance throughout human cultures, and the importance of the message, seem to be more than mere coincidence. It seems likely, a hunch confirmed by contemporary mystics, that the network of universal intelligence, seeking to encourage the development of our own intellectual, social, and spiritual progress, and to give us courage and hope for the tempestuous days of the transition ahead, has already communicated with us by broadcasting concentrated thought, a powerful telepathic action, perhaps aided by technology, or produced through the cooperative efforts of many highly advanced individuals, even entire populations acting in concert.

I believe telepathic messages of guidance and hope have been received by unusually sensitive and spiritual humans as visions and Divine messages since the dawn of our history. The "receivers" passed along the messages to members of their community. The communications were recognized as Divine inspiration and incorporated into their sacred beliefs. Naturally, different "receivers" and different cultures would interpret the message somewhat differently. The message itself may have changed slightly over the eons as the Divine intelligence evolved and grew. But the main thrust of the teaching was always hope for the future.

The Messianic promise holds the answer to the ultimate destiny of our civilization. Believing that we will win through the Messianic transition to the New World is the optimist's view. It is more than just opinion, it is an act of courage. It takes courage to insist that we will survive the power we've stolen from nature, that we will survive our political crises, our burgeoning population, our short-sightedness, our greed and aggressiveness. It takes courage to make it more than an act of hope and faith, but a call for action, a goal for a lifetime. I believe that regardless of what you and I do, humanity will survive the Messianic transition. But the individual makes a difference. You and I can help shorten the time of troubles, and speed the day when our civilization contacts the universe's other life forms and becomes part of the universal intelligence. As Theodore Herzl said, "If you will it, it isn't just an ideal."

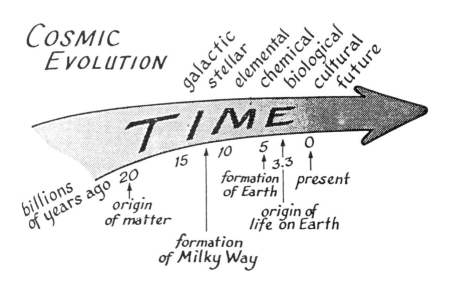

THE TREE OF LIFE

How can God, Creator of All that Was, Is and Will Be, feel concerned with what each of us think and do during our short lifespan here on earth? Is it plausible for humans to believe that God actually cares about our personal behavior or needs?

This was the problem that Jewish philosophers and Kabbalistic mystics sought to solve throughout the middle ages.

Jews were not always vexed with this problem. In Biblical days, Jews didn't have to ask themselves if God cared for them as individuals. He was their father and their tribal leader. He moved continually through the lives of His people. He could even be bargained with as Abraham did on behalf of Sodom (Gen 18: 23-32) and as Moses did on behalf of the Jewish people when they built the golden calf (Exodus 32:7-14).

The Jewish people's feelings and perception of Deity changed under the influence of Greek thought. Greek philosophers had rebelled against the silliness of their own gods and goddesses. Greek gods seemed more than anything else to be like humans writ large, with all their faults writ larger still. But the philosophers had swung too far away from their traditional anthropomorphism, imagining instead a Deity who was not only eternal, and immaterial, but unchanging, omniscient, omnipotent, and the quintessence of love, justice, and all other admirable qualities. The result was something that could exist only as a mental construct: static perfection. The concept of Divine perfection appeals to the lazy side of humans. If God is perfect and unchanging, then humanity can be as unthinking and carefree as children, leaving the entire responsibility for the direction of their personal destinies, their planet, and the universe, to God.

Greek perfectionism hit the Jews at a time when the turmoil in their political and social life made them especially vulnerable to the blandishments of ideal philosophic orderliness. As the new ideas seeped into Jewish thought processes, they troubled traditional belief in individual responsibility and free will, but most significantly, they tore a gap in the sense of intimacy that Jews had enjoyed with God.

In the end Jewish rationalists accepted the gap between God and humanity in exchange for an intellectual appreciation of tidy rational universal laws. Many preserved the Greek emphasis on God's eternal, unchanging nature, while fudging on details. Jewish philosophers such as Rambam, Albo, Crescas, and Spinoza believed that God always acted in a rational way and could be understood rationally, if one had the ability to do this. Other philosophers were bold enough to challenge and eliminate some of the Greek attributes of God in the name of higher Biblical truth.

However, on the basis of their own mystical experience, the Kabbalists refused to accept the gap between God and humanity. They came to accept the Greek rationalist perspective of YHVH as not only eternal and perfect but the formless, unchanging Ein Sof, the Infinite One. However, they developed a theory of their own which bridged the gap between humanity and God. The Kabbalists said that, while the Ein Sof is indeed infinite, incomprehensible, and unapproachable, the act of creation took place through a series of ten emanations (usually called ספירות Sefirot) descending from God to the finite world. Spiritually developed human beings are capable of making contact with the emanations close to the finite world, especially with מלכות Malkut, the tenth Sefirah which is directly responsible for the creation of the finite world. The theory itself is intellectual, and in its various ramifications very abstruse, but its foundation lies in the Kabbalistic certainty, born of mystical experience, that intimate contact with the Divine is possible.

Since the Sefirot are emanations of the Divine, the study of the Sefirot is the study of God, or at least as much of God as humans can comprehend. At the same time, it is the study of the creation of the finite universe. The Kabbalists say to Greek rationalism, finite creatures *can* know God, but, they admit, only as Creator. His essential Being (The Ein Sof) is always beyond us, but His activities (creation) can be observed and understood. They noted when Moses begged of God, "Please show me your glory," even he was told: "I will make all my goodness pass before you... but you cannot see my face for no man shall see me and live... You shall see me from behind, but you shall not see my face" (Exodus 33:18-23).

As a means of fitting Greek rationalism into traditional Jewish beliefs, the theory is excellent. Its central problem is that the emanations themselves are difficult to understand. The ten of them progress in descending order of holiness to the finite world. Different theorists have used different imagery to suggest their nature. Frequently they have been described as concentric circles, or with the shape of the Menorah in the temple (Exodus 25:31-37), or portrayed as a tree growing from the sky.

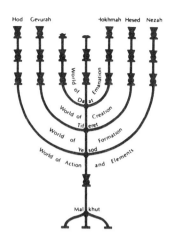

The ten Sefirot are also commonly pictured superimposed on the figure of a bisexual human prototype, אדם הקדמון Adam Hakadmon, in an attempt to signify their relationship to humanity. The superimposed picture shows the Sefirah of יסוד Yesod placed over the genitals of Adam Hakadmon. Yesod, the ninth Sefirah, is also called the foundation of צדיק Tsaddik, the Righteous One. The position of Yesod alludes to the creative energy of sexual reproducation as a driving force in the evolution of our physical environment, and as a creative force in lifting us to touch the Shekinah. (See "The Shekinah: She as God")

Even when they are portrayed as spheres, the Sefirot are not to be imagined as actual physical circles radiating outward from a point or collapsing inward. The word Sefirah sounds like the Greek word *sphere,* but it really comes from the Hebrew word *sappir* which is related to the English word *saphire* and like it signifies a gem of some kind.

The selection of the word *sappir* to refer to the emanations comes from the Torah's account of Moses, Aaron, and the 72 elders of Israel climbing Mount Sinai and seeing the God of Israel. Under His feet they saw something like a whitish sappir or a brick of sappir (the Hebrew translates either way) which was like the essense of the heavens in purity or clarity (Exodus 24: 10). The ambiguity of this important passage stems from its attempt to explain a mystical experience in a few words. Each of the Hebrew words in the passage has several possible meanings, but the word *sappir* is the most ambiguous of all. The multiple ambiguity of the separate words is responsible for the likelihood of finding 6-8 different interpretations of this passage in a half dozen different translations of the Bible.

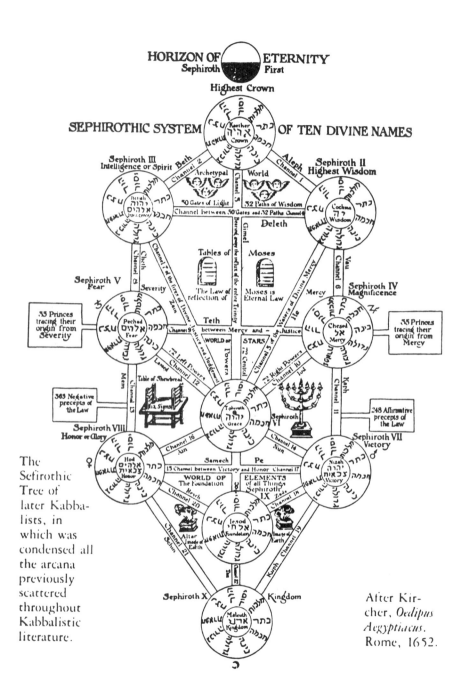

HORIZON OF ETERNITY

Sephiroth First

Highest Crown

SEPHIROTHIC SYSTEM OF TEN DIVINE NAMES

The Sefirothic Tree of later Kabbalists, in which was condensed all the arcana previously scattered throughout Kabbalistic literature.

After Kircher, *Oedipus Aegyptiacus.* Rome, 1652.

170

In addition to Sefirot, the emanations have also been described as lights, crowns, stages, garments, and mirrors. Personally, I prefer the concept of stages מדרגות (*madregot*), but since the term *Sefirot* is already so well known in English, I will use this term.

Greek rationalistic philosophers were absolutists. A concept was either true or false. Something either was or it was not. It moved or it didn't. Kabbalists were relativists, saying that often seeming contradictions are not opposite in kind but different only in degree. A Jew in New York faces east when praying. Another in Australia faces west. In Leningrad a Jew will face south when praying, and in South Africa, Jews pray to the north. But in whichever direction they turn, they are all facing toward Jerusalem.

Modern science confirms the Kabbalists' intuition. Conflicting truths can each be true. Physicists tell us that light is both a wave and a particle. Heisenberg's theory of uncertainty in modern quantum mechanics and Gudel's proof in modern mathematics also support the Kabbalistic view of reality.

The theory of the Sefirot maintains that the difference between the Infinite Deity and the finite creation is not the difference between opposites but rather the result of different variations in quantity. A solid and a liquid and a gas all seem to be different in quality. However, apply heat to the ice, and it will dissolve into a liquid. Apply more heat and the liquid will expand into a gas. The differences in the substances really are only a function of their structure and the quantity of energy in the molecules. In a similar way, Kabbalists say, creation evolves step by step from the Ein Sof to the transitory finite universe in which we live.

Most English books on the Kabbalah are largely devoted to an attempt to relate in detail the various Kabbalistic speculations on the nature of the Sefirot and their relation to each other. This approach to Kabbalistic study is like devoting months · of study to understand the laws of physics governing the internal combustion engine prior to learning how to drive. To drive one needs to (1) know the traffic laws; (2) practice driving; (3) obtain a road map showing how to get one's destination. The laws of physics relating to the engine are interesting, but they will make more sense after one has already had the experience of driving and knows something about cars.

Similarly, in order to begin practicing Kabbalistic mysticism, we need to perform mitzvot, which function as the traffic laws of human behavior. The Torah is like a road map guiding us on our journey through life. Prayer and meditation parallels the experience of driving. The abstruse study of the Sefirot takes us beyond the practice of prayer and meditation to an investigation of how and why we are propelled through life.

Although the image of Adam Hakadmon, the prototype human, is the most popular of the images in discussing the Sefirot, the image that I find most useful is that of the Tree of Life. The image of Adam Hakadmon is static. The tree however suggests growth. The Torah mentions two trees (Genesis 2:19): The Tree of the Knowledge of Good and Evil, and the Tree of Life. When we evolved into human beings, we consumed the fruit of the Tree of the Knowledge of Good and Evil.

But we have not yet tasted the fruit of the Tree of Life. This is because moral knowledge is passed on from generation to generation through culture. But knowledge of life has to be gained from the direct experience of living. This means that no one else can consume the fruit of the Tree of Life for us. The image of the tree is particularly apt because trees live longer than any other living thing on earth. There are trees still alive that were young saplings when Moses was a young man. The planting of trees is a symbol of faith in the future since it takes many years before they will grow big enough to provide shade and fruit.

The Torah is a Tree of Life for those who hold onto it. Those who are happy are described as well watered trees. With this wealth of association, a tree makes an excellent symbol for use in meditation, to help discover and direct one's spiritual growth. The following meditation is recommended for those who want to make a beginning in Kabbalistic mysticism:

Find a quiet place, close your eyes, and picture a tree. For this exercise it is important that you do not picture a real tree of your acquaintance. Instead imagine a tree. Once you have the general picture, focus on the root system. Observe how the roots sink into the ground. Are they widespread? Do they reach deep into the earth? Are they thick or thin? Do they intertwine and grope around rocks? Or are they straight and smooth?

When the tree's root system is clear in your mind, shift your attention to the trunk. Study it carefully. Look at the bark and the thickness of the trunk. Will the trunk sway in the wind? Is it strong? Does it have a hollow in it? Is it tall or short. straight or twisted, single or forked?

From the trunk let your eyes follow the curves of the branches. Do they reach out or upward or droop to earth? Are the branches straight, curved or gnarled? Are there many or few? Are they growing or dying? Do animals inhabit the branches of your tree? Do you want them to?

Now focus your attention on your tree's leaves. Are there many or few? Are the leaves round or pear shaped or thin? Are they green or brown? Are the edges serrated or smooth? Are they healthy looking or falling off the tree?

Do not read any farther until you have tried this exercise, preferably three or four times. Then return to this chapter and continue.

Once you have examined your imagined tree in detail and have decided exactly how it looks, you may use your image as a diagnostic tool and as a prescriptive vehicle for spiritual development.

The four parts of the tree (roots, trunk, branches, and leaves) represent four parts of our spiritual personality. The roots represent your spiritual ties to tradition. If you are deeply rooted into your family's traditions, your roots will be deep and thick. If you feel alienated and marginal in your relationship to the religious and cultural community of your people, your roots will be weak, small or shallow. Roots that encircle rocks indicate tenacity in the face of adverse experience.

The trunk represents your own individual will power and your conscious decisions about spiritual growth. The bark of the tree like the skin of the body transmits sensations and feelings. A thick-barked tree suggests a person who is self-directed and confident, able to draw on inner resources. A thin-barked tree indicates a person who is more sensitive to others and to the environment. Whose social manner is gentle and tender.

The branches represent your interactions with other people. Spiritual development is strongly influenced by the ability to reach out to other humans and to intertwine with them. If the branches are short and stumpy or twisted, you are not reaching out to the world around you sufficiently. Straight branches represent constant relationships. Twisting branches represent relationships that undergo sharp changes in direction and intensity.

The tree's foliage represents your openness to spiritual energies from above. Many leaves, as well as leaves that are very green, represent receptivity to God's nourishment. Falling leaves or a tree whose leaves are sparce suggest you have turned away from the radiant light of God's presence.

Having analyzed your imaginary tree, which is really the projection of your own spiritual self, you can now proceed to develop your spiritual self through meditative exercise on the "Tree of Life." The Torah is referred to as a tree of life because it is a prescription for living in a way that makes life rich and satisfying. The mitzvot are the details of a behavioral system which influences your spiritual growth subtly but steadily. Meditating on the "Tree of Life" enables you to consciously direct the future of your life.

Both the behavioral discipline of the mitzvot and the conscious discipline of meditative exercise are necessary. To work on your spiritual development with the "Tree of Life" meditation, it is necessary to devote at least ten to fifteen minutes once or twice a week in addition to every Shabbat.

First concentrate on the image of your tree and then consciously identify yourself with the tree so that you come to feel that the roots, trunk, branches, and leaves *are* you. Then, by picturing appropriate changes in the tree, you can start growing in the direction you desire. You can extend your roots, grow new upward reaching branches, enlarge your leaves and deepen their color, thicken or thin the bark of your trunk, and make the trunk itself more flexible or sturdy.

As the tree grows and prospers in your mind, you yourself will be developing spiritually. After a few months of doing this spiritual exercise faithfully and simultaneously observing an increased number of mitzvot, you will find that the direction of your life will change and you will experience spiritual uplifting.

THE FIRST STEP IN JEWISH SPIRITUAL LIFE *

This manual intends to give you practical information in the area of spiritual discipline and resources. You are required to spend at least a half hour each day, and an additional two hours each week, at this work. You will have to be honest with yourself. You cannot do this work alone. You need a trusted friend, with whom you can work together, and with whom you can freely discuss your work. Spiritual work in loneliness, without the possibility of sharing and comparing, can be harmful. Be prepared to let the work affect you fully, and take you into its own direction. Be prepared to have your mode of living profoundly changed in all its aspects. Read this manual time and time again. Do not proceed with one exercise, before you have the first one under full control and can at will duplicate it at any time you desire.

If you do follow this guide honestly and conscientiously, it will not take you all the way. It will only introduce you to some elementary techniques of the spiritual laboratory. When you will have reached the last of the exercises in your own practical experience, and when you can 'control' your actions as outlined here, you will need a teacher and guide to prescribe the specific and very personal other steps for you. Let me assure you that there are teachers who can take you farther. Further steps cannot be given to you in a manual, since it cannot speak to your own specific differences from other people. Your own very individual further development will need individual guiding.

But for you, your own progress will be the decisive factor. You will soon come to realize that in order to make progress in this work, a certain level-headed sobriety is immensely necessary. *Anyone thinking that rapture awaits him instead of hard work, will soon be disappointed.*

This does not mean that you will not get anywhere. It does mean that your real effort will be rewarded.

It is thus intended as a laboratory guide, to help you on your way. In

---

* This is a selection from material prepared by M'shulam Zalman son of Haya Gitil. Rabbi Schachter teaches at Temple University, Philadelphia, Pa.

order to keep you from confusion, it is suggested that for the time being, you stop your further reading in this area. Later on, when you will have some real experience behind you, further reading will prove to be a joy instead of a hindrance. The many states described will be familiar to you, and serve as further validation of the rightness of your own experience. But until you gain positive experience, refrain from further reading, in order to find the way.

On the other hand inspirational reading (instead of how-to-do-it) is of immense importance. Find time (it need not be very much — in this you suit yourself to your own schedule and inclination) and hold on to this time as something very precious. Address God and ask Him that your reading may inspire your continued effort. Then read for a while.

Many prayers have been offered for your success.

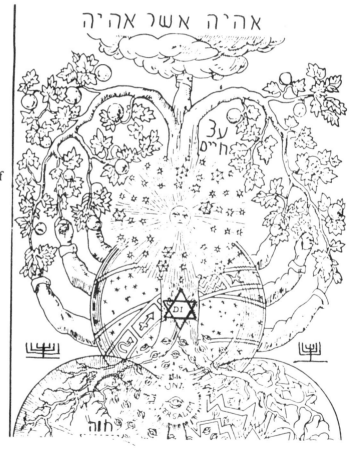

אהי׳ה אשר אהי׳ה

The Tree of
Knowledge of
Good & Evil
Altona, 1785.

ON MEDITATION

You want to grow spiritually, grow a soul. The Zohar has it, "Each one is given a Nephesh" (meaning the lowest of the five soul stages. The others are Ru'ach, N'shamah, Chayah, Y'chidah. Nephesh corresponds to the action aspect, Ru'ach to the emotive, and N'shamha to the intellective.). "If one so merits, (by refining oneself), one is granted Ru'ach, etc."

This Nephesh can become a functioning and active force within you, but it has to be roused. The best way to rouse 'Nephesh' is meditation (because it shifts your identity from the body to Nephesh), coupled with the active observance of the Mitzvot (because it asserts itself as the 'self' in the active fulfilment). Perhaps you have tried to meditate. Do this now. Take ten minutes for meditation. Meditate upon God. Continue your reading later. Go on, meditate, and put the book away!

Being honest with yourself, you will have observed several things:

1. You had some trouble finding enough material to think about.

2. You were beset by many distractions.

There are, of course, a large number of 'outer' distractions, such as sounds, sights, and other sense impressions, that want to keep claiming your attention. You can look for a quiet spot, find yourself a comfortable chair, and close your eyes. But having done this, your other troubles seem to begin. There is an onrush of thoughts and inner sensations. Before closed eyes a host of images seem to present themselves. You hear yourself breathe and you may even sense your heartbeat. You remember all sorts of trite things you must do. (For this it is best to keep a pad and pencil at your side, and to write these down for after your spiritual work period.) You feel all sorts of itches and twitches. It is quite difficult to settle your mind.

It will become important at a later stage to do something about these distractions, but for the time being the problem of content is the more important one. What did you meditate on?

You have read about God's immanence, His indwelling in creation, it is called His being m'malleh Kol Almin, His filling of all the worlds with Light and Life. If you are acquainted with some literature on this point, make it your business to study it again, and learn to rethink it in sequence. If you are not, the following might be of help: psalm 104 and 147.

At first you study the thought and you do this in an academic, objective way. You want to fully understand the entire image, to its very last detail.

However, when you have mastered the thought sequence in detail and in richness, you must give it all a twist into another dimension, that of situational thinking. Let me give you two illustrations: You can, for instance, study the toxic effects of carbon monoxide on the various cells. You learn to understand in great detail the process of the poisoning, which makes it impossible for the vital organs to keep functioning. The patient dies. Now the twist from the conceptual mode to the situational mode occurs when you realize that it is not air that you breathe, but carbon monoxide, and that you are about to die. This situational mode of thought, we shall henceforth call Ada-ata D'nafshey thinking. It fills you with an immediate emotional awareness, in this case, with horror and anxiety. It also produces behavior, in this case escaping behavior.

Or, as another example: You can fully understand what a large sum of money could mean to someone. The beneficiary can do many things he could not do up to now. You can picture the economic and social effects of a sudden acquisition of money. Now you twist that Ada'ata D'nafshey, and you are the beneficiary. You are filled with an emotion of enlargement and this too begets behavior — in this case approach behavior.

All this is applicable to meditation. All meditation that has gone beyond the sequence thinking stage ought to be Ada-ata D'nafshey thinking.

So you meditate on God filling this universe with life and you do this Ada-ata D'nafshey — you are now, here filled with Life — with God. When you finally face this tremendous fact, you feel something in your heart. But the feeling is not as important as whom you feel. When you have reached that point in your meditation, fasten on to it for a few moments. Nothing, neither your thought sequence nor your emotional response is as important as He whom you are facing and who fills you with Life. So hold on to this confrontation for a while. When you do this, you need not do anything else except face and behold Him.

You may want to do this only once or twice and then to proceed to another thought. But here you must be cautioned. There is no benefit in rushing ahead. You must work on this one thought for at least twenty times. If you do this more often, you will benefit even more.

Of course you will have problems. You might become bored by the one thought, but this only shows that you have not sufficiently deepened your thinking. How many times have you indulged Ada-ata D'nafshey in some non-spiritual thought and desire and did not get bored by it? It won't do to move on. This moving on from thought, this kind of scanning can give you only information. Meditation is precisely the working with the information you already have.

One can really live a whole life with just one meditation. So you subdue the boredom — and here is where it becomes work — until you break through. You will know that you have broken through by the fact that your subconscious has, in this area, become slightly reoriented. Life, filling the all, will have become a real factor in your living.

SHIVITIH AND KAVVANAH
God's Presence and Your Intention

You have learned how to meditate on God's Immanence, and his indwelling is now a part of your mental and emotional life. You now wish to place your functional life in His Presence. You want to be able to practice the Presence of God. This discipline will become the mainstay of your spiritual life. This is not too difficult at first, but it does take remembering. You will from time to time remember that you stand before Him. You sort of wink at Him, while engaged in whatever function you are busy with. You eat and enjoy your food, and you remember Him. You might recite a blessing over the food. It need not take long, a short moment is all that is necessary.

Let me explain to you the function of כונה Kavvanah. Kavvanah means intention. Our intention is always free. There is nothing that can obstruct your intending. Even if the whole world coerces you into a pattern of actions, you can always 'intend' whatever you want. For instance, you sit in the dentist's chair. He drills and you feel a sting of pain, but you can 'intend' this pain as an offering of love. You offer to God the moment of pain, intending to suffer it for Him. You might put it in somewhat this way: "Ribono Shel Olam! — You are good and Your universe is good. The all is filled with Your mercy and goodness, as is the pain I feel. I cannot bring You any other sacrifice. Please accept this moment of pain as a love offering from me." Or you work in your day by day endeavor. You do whatever you must do, and you intend: "God of Law and Order. You have ordained work for man. In doing — I intend to do Your will. I wish to cleave to You in this action." Or you travel and time is taken up by it. You lean back and wink at Him in your mind as if to say "Sweet Father, I enjoy Your presence! The rhythm of the wheels, the fleeting scenery, are all nothing but You. You contain me and my vehicle. I will be careful in travel, for this is Your will. Guard my going out and my coming back. I am secure in You."

You see these 'arrows of awareness' are rather simple to practice. You will soon find that placing yourself in His Presence will come with some practice.

Especially when engaged in doing a Mitzvah, you will want to put your intention to use. On the Sabbath, when eating, you can intend לכבוד השבת "Likhvod Hashabbath — May I eat this food and enjoy it for Your sake, for this is the Mitzvah of the Shabbat."

When putting on the T'fillin, or lighting the candles, you can intend: "Lovely Lord, take my body as an instrument of Your will. My limbs are prepared, and are at Your disposal. Use them!" and then you say the blessing.

It is helpful to have a visual image in the Kavvanah. You picture the Will of God flowing into your body and soul, becoming united with the limbs, organs, senses, brain and nerves, and moving — make sure at this point to feel them moving by His will — to execute the Mitzvah. This should become well familiar to you. Do not go on to the next point until the practice of Kavvanah has become firmly established in your habit pattern.

ON THE EXAMINATION OF ONE'S CONSCIENCE AND GOING TO SLEEP

Before going to sleep start out by fully and completely forgiving anyone who wronged or hurt you, and pray for the welfare of that person. Continue by affirming the Oneness of God, and your longing to love Him and then read the Sh'ma.

Finally take a short tally of your actions during the day. Begin with the first thought upon awakening. (This thought is of tremendous power, it exerts influence on the rest of the day. Make sure to think a good first thought and last thought every day.) Don't spend more than five minutes on this tally to begin with. Just check through your actions to see if they are as you planned them. If you are sure that you did not do the right thing, hold the thought, word or action up to God, and with a short arrow prayer, ask Him to remove this kind of thing from your life. Again, much will depend on the sobriety and tenacity you will show every night.

Once a week, (Thursday night might be best) you must set aside more time than usual, and do this when you are still fresh. If you leave this until you are too worn out, you cannot expect to succeed. Therefore plan the evening accordingly. Let us say you are now alone, and not too tired. At first you slip into the 'Life' meditation, and then when you come to feel His Presence in your being, begin to judge yourself in His sight, not harshly, not carelessly, but justly. Do this in great detail, and look at your motivations in detail. Don't condemn or convict yourself, but visualize yourself before God, and listen to His judgment.

Then offer all your 'sins' and guilts up to Him. Ask Him to take these from you and wash you clean. You need at this point an image in which you can bring yourself to arouse His Infinite Mercy. This arousing of God's Mercy is called Hith'or'ruth Rach'mim Rabbim. Each person finds himself comfortable in his own image. You may find one of the following useful: The prince, all dirty, facing his Father the King — The image of the prisoner, who is made to help his oppressors — The image of the spark which wants to return to the flame, but is bottled up — The image of the prince, who, in love with a princess, (or vice versa) has been robbed of the hard earned money, saved penny by penny, for ransoming the beloved — the image of the child who has lost his parents in the crowd because he looked at some puppies in the window — The image of the amnesiac, exiled prince, who suddenly remembers that he is a prince.

The purpose of this image is for you to feel the need of His Mercy, to feel so helpless in His Presence and out of your inability to do anything to help yourself that you implore Him in your own language. This utter helplessness before God is not a theological dogma but a functional attitude appropriate for this moment of your spiritual development. Identify with one of these and implore Him for mercy. Make sure to use everyday language in doing this.

Now, at this point, you might step into the even higher motive of being sorry for what you have done to Him. How you abused His Presence and Life in you, in order to do the very opposite of His plan of love for you, how you took His very Head and Heart and soiled Them foolishly. How you are more pained for what you did to your Beloved, than for the reversal of your own progress — Read perhaps one of Psalms 6, 25, 51, 73, or 130, a few times. Then renew your covenant with Him and prepare for bed.

When you are all ready for sleep, lift as it were your soul in your hands and give it to Him, saying the words: "In Thy Hand do I hide my soul — for the night. Thou hast — doest, and wilt redeem me. God of Truth." Visualize your tensions walking out of you — one by one, beginning from your toes — become all limp — out from between your eyes. At last, repeating the verse, and asking Him to wake you refreshed at — o'clock, and to take over your breathing and rest, feeling at the same time caressed by His Hand — visualize your mattress as His Arms.

On other nights, after the short examination, screen yourself in from sounds and cares by visualizing an angel — a spiritual force field — of Grace at your right, this force field being impenetrable by care and worry; at your left, screened off by an angel of power and strength; before you, an angel of soft light and luminousness; and behind you, an angel of healing. Over your head picture the very Presence of the loving God. As you visualize this, you say:

"In the name of יהוה
the God of Israel:
at my right hand Michael
at my left Gabriel
ahead of me Oriel
behind me Raphael
above my head the שכינה
Shekenah of God!"

Imagine yourself plugging into Michael for love, — so that you can love more the next day — Gabriel for strength, to fill you for the next day, — Oriel with the light of the mind, — Raphael with healing for all your ills.

Again let me ask you not to give up. These are new practices which you must acquire, and their real power begins to show well only after you can control the sequence of thought and feeling. The first time it may come a bit easier, but after that it takes a great deal of persistence. You are rebuilding some intangibles inside yourself. Years of habitual drivenness must be fought, but you will succeed, if you persist. Only then continue with the other points outlined here.

אַרְבָּעָה שֶׁנִּכְנְסוּ אֶל הַפַּרְדֵּס
אַרְבָּעָה שֶׁרָצוּ אֶל לְחַפֵּשׂ
לָדַעַת לִפְנֵי ״ב״ וּמִי בַּמָּרוֹם
וּמֵהֶם רַק עֲקִיבָא יָצָא בְּשָׁלוֹם.

(המבין יבין)

182

RECOMMENDED FOR FURTHER READING

Philip Berg, *Kabbalah for the Layman*
The Author, dean of the Research Center of Kabbalah, has written a modern style work to help us attain spiritual growth.

Jacob Bazak, *Judaism and Psychical Phenomena*
A study of esp and magic in Rabbinical Literature by an open minded and rational Jerusalem Judge.

David Blumenthal, *Understanding Jewish Mysticism*
Contains the full text of Sefer Yetsira and selections from Pirkei Heikhalot, and the Zohar, with a good commentary by Rabbi Blumenthal.

Ben Zion Bokser, *The Jewish Mystical Tradition*
A collection of mystical texts from the Bible to the twentieth century, with a fine introduction by a good modern scholar.

Martin Buber, *For the Sake of Heaven*
A novel relating the attempts of several Hasidic Rabbis to influence the outcome of the Napoleonic Wars through the use of Kabbalah power.

Seymour Cohen, *The Holy Letter: A Study in Medieval Jewish Sexual Morality*
A fine translation of a short 13th century Kabbalistic work.

Moses Cordovero, *The Palm Tree of Deborah*
A short 16th century summary of the Lurianic Kabbalah view of human saintliness.

Joel Dobin, *To Rule both Day and Night*
A Reform Rabbi who is also an astrologer presents the original sources of astrology in the Midrash and the Talmud.

Louis Jacobs, *Jewish Mystical Testimonies*
An anthology of 20 mystical texts with an excellent introduction and commentary on each one by Rabbi Jacobs.

Aryeh Kaplan, *The Bahir*
A fine introduction and commentary to a very important 12th century text by a scholar who is a true Baal Teshuvah.

Joseph Klausner, *The Messianic Idea in Israel*
A good treatment of the sources in the Bible and the Talmud by a non-Messianist.

Abraham Kook, *The Lights of Penitence etc.*
Three major works, several essays, and poems, by the Chief Rabbi of Israel (1919-1935). He saw the holy sparks even in the Secular Zionist Pioneers.

Levi Krakovsky, *Kabbalah: The Light of Redemption*
Like most of the books issued by the Research Center of Kabbalah this is authentically orthodox, but unrelated to modern thought styles and therefore difficult to appreciate.

Moshe Chaim Luzzato, *Way of God*
A classic statement of major kabbalistic principles. Vocalized Hebrew text with English translation by Aryeh Kaplan. Also a Research Center type.

David Meltzer, *The Secret Garden*
A high quality anthology of two dozen selections; many from 17th-19th century Kabbalists. Lacking in commentary or modern interpretation.

Raphael Patai, *The Messiah Texts*
A fine collection of messianic speculations from Isaiah to Herzl with an introduction and commentary by a modern scholar who is also a Messianist. A basic book for anyone who wants to read the "signs" of the times.

Roy Rosenberg, *The Anatomy of God*
A very good translation of four books from the Zohar. It is much superior to "The Kabbalah Unveiled," by Mather.

Abraham Rothberg, *The Sword of the Golem*
A novel, based on further aspects of the Golem legend, exploring the theme "a time for peace and a time for war."

Alexandre Safran, *The Kabbalah; Law and Mysticism in the Jewish Tradition*
The author shows clearly why just presenting the metaphysical theories of the 10 Sefirot without stressing Israel as God's chosen people and observance of mitsvot, is a distortion.

Gershom Scholem, is the world's greatest scholar in Jewish Mysticism. His books are authentic, academic, and not very inspirational; yet they can be very rewarding in helping weed out the tendency of many writers to read Hindu, Bhuddist, Occult and Christian mystical concepts into Kabbalah

Kabbalah
A collection of articles taken from the Encyclopedia Judaica. This is a handy reference to specific topics and personalities.

The Messianic Idea in Judaism
A series of essays on Jewish spirituality; the most important of them being "Redemption Through Sin," and "Devekut, or Communion with God."

Major Trends in Jewish Mysticism
A very academic history of Jewish mysticism.

On the Kabbalah and its Symbolism
Five essays; the best one being "The Idea of Golem."

Zohar
Selected readings from the Zohar. It is the best introduction to Kabbalistic texts. Unfortunately, Scholem does not comment on the texts.

Abba Hillel Silver, *A History of Messianic Speculation in Israel*
Recounts the methods and failures of all those who have tried to calculate the "end" or become the Messiah.A good warning for contemporary Messianists lacking in humility.

Zalman Schachter, *Fragments of a Future Scroll*
Reb Zalman is one of the best teachers of Hasidic and Kabbalistic ways in the world today. I have used his "First Step in Jewish Spiritual Life" in this book. If you can go to Temple U. in Philadelphia and sit at his feet you will be blessed.

Herbert Weiner, *$9\frac{1}{2}$ Mystics*
Encounters with 9 contemporary mystics and Kabbalists, by a Reform Rabbi who is halfway there.

Elie Wiesel, *Messengers of God, Souls on Fire*
Two books about God intoxicated Jews, by a modern literary prophet.

Gershon Winkler, *Dybbuk*
Six well dramatized accounts of Soul Possession and exorcism, plus a study of the Soul before and after life.

NOT RECOMMENDED

Edward Albertson, *Understanding the Kabbalah*
Author of books on the I Ching, Yoga, Zen, Vedanta and seances; he must read 20 books on a subject and then write one himself.

Aleister Crowley, *777 and Other Qubalistic Writings*
He reads his occult doctrines of numerology, astrology and magic into and out of everything.

Migene Gonzales-Wippler, *A Kabbalah for the Modern World*
He has a fairly good chapter on the Tree of Life, but his explanations of God, Sex and Creation are distorted by his occult prejudices.

Stephan Hoeller, *The Royal Road*
A distorted interpretation of Kabbalah through Tarot cards and other superstitions.

Charles Ponce, *Kabbalah*
Nicely ilustrated, it has several sensitive and insightful parts, but it too often distorts kabbalistic teaching by forcing parallels to Hindu Yogic concepts.

Leo Sehaya, *The Universal Meaning of the Kabbalah*
Although the author is Jewish, he distorts Kabbalah through Christian concepts and images.

A. E. Waite, *The Holy Kabbalah*
A theosophist who depended on a poor French translation. He provides some gems amidst the gravel.

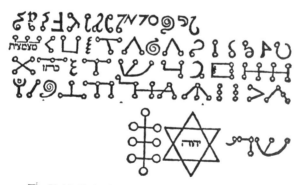

The Kabbalistic alphabet. The letters bear an uneasy resemblance to Hebrew characters but end in ringlets with rounded corners. (*Sefer Raziel p.* 44*b*).

WHICH KABBALAH?

Kabbalah is one of those words that seems to have a half-dozen different spellings and just as many meanings. The following are the designations most often found in books on the subject:

Kabbalah usually refers to the Jewish mystical tradition which has emphasized prayer, and study of esoteric commentaries on the Torah.

Cabala is the spelling usually employed when discussing the spread of kabbalistic teachings and symbols into Christian circles during the Renaissance.

Qabalah most often refers to the magical/occult use of the Kabbalah beginning in the mid-1800s.

*   *   *   *

The human mind is very adept at finding patterns hidden in the complexity of nature. This is the basis for Science, Religion, History and Economics. But the human mind often finds patterns where they do not exist. This is the basis for Magic, Superstition, Prejudice and much New Age Thinking. This book begins with a pattern that is true, and ends with one that is false. *(The Kanizsa square below is an illusion)*. If you have read and understood my teaching you will be SAFE from error. The cognoscent will comprehend.

I went out, Lord
People were coming and going,
Walking and running.
Everything was rushing: cars, trucks, the
    street, the whole town.
People were rushing not to waste time,
To catch up with time, To gain time.

Good-bye, excuse me, I haven't time.
I'll come back, I can't wait, I haven't time.
I'd love to help you, but I haven't time.
I can't accept, having no time.
I can't think, I can't read, I'm swamped,
    I haven't time.
I'd like to pray, but I haven't time.

You understand, Lord, they simply haven't the time

The children are playing, they haven't time
    right now . . . Later on . . .
The students have homework to do, they haven't
    time . . . Later on . . . .
The young marrieds have their house, they have
    to fix it up.
They haven't the time . . . Later on . . .
They are dying, they were going to give, but . . .
Too late! . . . They have no more time!

And so, all people run after time, Lord

They pass through life running, hurried,
    jostled, overburdened,
Frantic, and they never get there. They still
    haven't time.
In spite of all their efforts they're still
    short of time,
Lord, you must have made a mistake
There is a big mistake somewhere.

The hours are too short,
The days are too short.
Our lives are too short,
O Lord, why don't we have enough time.
Time for our parents and our children.
Time to study and learn.
Time to think and to pray.
Time to visit the sick and lonely.
Time to **do** *the Mitzvot we think of.*
Time to appreciate the blessings we have.

Lord, You who are beyond time, You smile to
    see us fighting it.
You know what You are doing.
You make no mistakes in Your distribution of
    time to people.
You give each one of us time to do what **we**
    really want to do.
So we must not deface time,
Waste time, Kill time,

For time is a gift that You give us,
But a perishable gift,
A gift that does not keep.
Lord, I have time,

I have plenty of time,
The years of my life,
The days of my years,
The hours of my days,
They are all mine, to use now in order to sanctify time.

Mine to fill quietly with Shabbat and Yom Tov.
Mine to fill completely with Torah and Mitzvot.
So when the end of my time comes,
I can say I did what I should have done,
I had enough time.

.Adapted from Michael Quoist

Creation.

When you intend to approach the Creator...

KABBALAH MANUALA FOR RABBI ALLEN MALLER
CHARLES SHERMAN